notes

1. what do you believe is the power to become

becoming mature Christians / Sons of god

Caterpillar to the butterfly / Metamorphosis

POWER TO BECOME

POWER TO BECOME

By
Dr. Cornelius Sanders II, Ph.D.

Leathers Publishing
4500 College Blvd.
Leawood, KS 66211
Phone: 1 / 888 / 888-7696

Unless otherwise noted, all scripture quotations are from the Authorized King James version of the Bible.

Copyright 2000
Printed in the United States

Second Printing 2006

ISBN: 1-58597-023-9

Library of Congress Catalog Card No. 00-90068

4500 College Blvd.
Overland Park, KS 66211
Phone: 1/888-888-7696

FOREWORD

IT IS A MOST HUMBLED and honorable privilege to be called and received as a Father in the Faith by other God-ordained sons.

My son in the Faith, Dr. Cornelius Sanders, is a gift from God to the family of God. Cornelius is a devoted husband whose love for his wife is always evident and a proud father whose dedication has also been present. He is such a humble shepherd who knows what it is to be committed to the Lord and connected to His people. I thank God for trusting me with a brother in the Lord, friend for life, and a son in the Faith.

If the Body of Christ is to ever reach our full potential, growth, development and maturity, then it is of utmost importance that we come to understand "Power To Become."

It is my delight, therefore, to commend to the Christian family this life-transforming book by one of the most insightful men in recent years, Cornelius Sanders. This book captures, in my opinion, the very essence of the high calling of God. Hebrews 3:1 gives us the heavenly calling, which is salvation. II Timothy 1:9 describes the holy calling of sanctification. But Philippians 3:14 tells us to press for the prize of the high calling, and that is Sonship.

"Power To Become" creates a sincere hunger for the High Calling, to grow up and become a maturing son of the Father. Borrowing the Air Force slogan, "Aim High," that this truly is the high calling of God — Aim for Sonship.

This book helps us to have a biblical perspective of

how the Father intends for his family to impact the world we live in by becoming what Jesus Christ ordained us to be.

It's all about him! And this book, "Power To Become," teaches us how to become more and more like Him. Better still, how to allow Christ to be who He is in us.

I trust that you will not just enjoy this book, and I am certain that you will, but more importantly, be transformed by it.

Dr. Nate Holcomb
Bishop and Pastor
Christian House of Prayer
It's All About Him Ministies
Covenant Connection International

CONTENTS

INTRODUCTION

In Matthew chapter 24:14 it talks about the gospel of the kingdom being preached. Well, I give this revelation to the body of Christ and to all of God's creation. I do not give this as the end of a thing, but as the beginning of a thing. Not as though I am the only one that God has talked to along these lines, but as one who has a mandate from heaven to share publicly what has been given to me privately. The Bible says freely we have received, freely we give. In other words, share what you have.

A few years ago the Lord began to deal with me on a subject. I did not try to preach it or teach it; I only meditated it, Joshua 1:8. Out of those few years it developed into what I am going to share. I believe that this will answer so many questions that we have in the church and why there have been delays on even some of our prayers. I believe that after you read this small part of what God has given me to contribute to the growth of the Body of Christ that it will change us and we will never be the same again. In JESUS' name, amen. So I present to you what has been given to me as we have entered into a new millennium and the 21st century, POWER TO BECOME.

* How does the author use the analogy of a
Caterpillar & butterfly to explore ones destiny?
{ The Caterpillar has no illusion, he knows it is his
destiny to fly.

2 What is the error a Christian makes?
Christian tries to do & become something through
their own devices instead of allowing god to do it

CHAPTER ONE

Making or Becoming

POWER TO BECOME — you can't make yourself a pastor, but you can become one if that's what God has called you to be. You can't make yourself one, but you can become. And there are so many things in life today that people are trying to make themselves be instead of realizing the one thing that God has called us to become. A caterpillar is born to fly. The caterpillar when it comes into the earth comes into the earth an ugly, creeping, crawling thing that most of us don't like to pick up or touch. Just to look at it makes chills go up and down our bodies. And as he inches along, he knows from the time of his birth that it is his destiny to become a butterfly. As the caterpillar inches along, everything and everyone is looking at it and frowning at it and talking about it. While all of that is going on, the caterpillar knows that it is his destiny to become. As soon as he entered the earth he is already becoming. You may not see it, but it is his destiny to fly. He may start in a lowly place, but God has given the caterpillar the power to become. He can only become what God has destined him to be, even though his beginnings look bad. No matter how much he would desire to try and be something else, he can't, but it is his destiny to become what God has purposed him to be in this life.

And so I want to deal with us on POWER TO BE-

1

COME. Not what are you trying to make yourself, but what has GOD given you the power to become. I believe that there is a higher calling than ministry; I believe that there is a higher position than a servant. Paul, one of what we would consider the greatest apostles of the new testament, said and proclaimed, decreed and declared according to the book of Romans 1:1, I Corinthians 1:1, Galatians 1:1, II Timothy 1:11, that he was an apostle, preacher, teacher and a servant of Jesus Christ, but in the later part of his ministry in the book of Philippians, chapter three, verses thirteen and fourteen, he said that he was still reaching for and pressing for the HIGH CALLING of God in Christ Jesus. So I submit to you that the high calling can't be an apostle or the five-fold ministry (which deals with servanthood) because Paul was already that, and most of us in Christendom think that the high calling is ministry. If that were the case, it would exclude over 90% of all Christians, and that is not the justice of God. So if it is not ministry, then it must be something that we can all arrive at. Everyone can arrive at the high call, and that's good news — hallelujah! Now we must remember that we have to press for it; let's get a little taste of what the Lord is saying to us.

✯ In the gospel of John 1:12 it reads, *But as many as received him (JESUS), to them gave he **power to become** the **sons of God**, even to them that believe on his name.* **SONSHIP** is the destiny of the believer, sonship is the ultimate place in the kingdom, sonship is the high calling of God in Christ Jesus, and God said that He has given you and me POWER TO BECOME SONS.

Now we must deal with all of this because God said that He gave us the power to become. That means we might not be yet, but we are inching along, and those of us that have the revelation of sonship know that one day we are going to fly; one day we are going to take off; one day we are going to be the sons that are in our Heavenly Father's heart and eyes. God is very patient with us as we inch along like the caterpillar trying to make ourselves something that we are not, instead of just becoming who we are.

One of the first questions that we have to ask ourselves is: do we believe on JESUS? If you do, you can start getting excited now because you are already on the right track and we must start there. God already knows your destiny; God already knows what you are supposed to be; we are the ones that have a problem with it. John 1:13 says, *Which were born, not of blood, nor of the will of the flesh, nor of the will of man, **but of God.***

★ According to John 1:12 how does a Christian become a son? - receive him & believe on him

★ The 3 phrases that ~~describe~~ describe Sonship - 1. Destiny of the believer
2. ultimate place in the kingdom
3. high calling of god in Christ Jesus

3

* two examples of people becoming sons in the old & New testaments.

{ Jacob - old testament
{ Paul - New testament

these two had to mature, grow up suffer
both were transformed & god changed their names.

---

why is the earth waiting on the sons of god?
A. sons make things happen in the earth
B. The earth is put back into proper ~~th~~ balance

How can the christian own thoughts hinder them from becoming a son?
A Focusing on superficial achievements
B Failure to realize god's power is needed to obtain sonship
C. cost of sonship too high (some Christians may think)

CHAPTER TWO

Accepted

SO MANY OF US are striving in life to be something that God never called us to be. We are trying to get everywhere but what God has spoken. We think that all these other things are the best places; oh, but God is revealing something about sonship, power to become sons. God knew that it was going to take power to get us out of our own thought, power to change us and get us out of stinken thinken, amen. Romans 8:19-22 says (paraphrase): *the whole earth the creation is groaning and waiting, expecting and looking for the manifestation or the revelation of the SONS of God.*

When sons arrive, the weather changes, the earth is groaning for us. The newscaster would say, "Oh, we have crazy weather over here and crazy weather over there," but the Bible says the earth is waiting on you because when you arrive you say peace and be still, hallelujah; sons do that. Sons are the ones that get things done in the earth.

Ephesians 1:1-6 reads, *Paul, an apostle of Jesus Christ by the will of God, to the saints which are at Ephesus, and to the faithful in Christ Jesus: Grace be to you, and peace, from God our Father, and from the Lord Jesus Christ. Blessed be the God and Father of our Lord Jesus Christ, who hath blessed us with all spiritual blessings in heavenly places in Christ: Accord-*

5

*ing as he hath **chosen us** in him **before the foundation** of the world, that we should be holy and without blame before him in love; Having **predestinated us** unto the **adoption of children** by Jesus Christ to himself, according to the **good pleasure of his will,** To the praise of the glory of his grace, wherein he hath made us **ACCEPTED in the beloved.***

In the book of Ruth, the book that talks about kissers and cleavers, leaving and cleaving, Boaz (who is a type of Christ, Ruth, chapter two) came to the field and asked the servant (which is a type of the local church pastor) that was set over the reapers (which are a type of the members in the local church), who is that lady (Ruth) in my field (visiting the local church)? The interesting thing is that the servant knew that she was there but did not at that time know her name. Boaz, when he showed up, took note of her instantly and asked about her and then went to her and told her to stick with me and don't look on another field; you are in the right place.

The point is the shepherd may overlook you; the members may overlook you, but God never overlooks you, amen. God said tat you are already accepted. If you are a Christian, God accepts YOU. So you don't have to do anything to be accepted in the eyes of God; you are already worthy and priceless; you are more valuable than the whole world. There is nothing that you have to do in His sight to be accepted.

Let me give you understanding of what I'm saying. I have two children, Antwone and Tiffany, both of whom are now grown. But when they were teenagers, they didn't always work as hard as we thought they could have worked, but they are accepted in my wife's and my sight. Because they are **MY** children I bless them, not because they hold some position or do

Christian does not have to work to be accepted

Salvation makes us accepted

6

everything right, but because they are my children I accept them. I tell my children all the time whether you play sports, play an instrument or do something great in school, be it drama club or the football team, it just does not matter whether you are on it or not on it. I STILL LOVE YOU, and there is nothing that you can do that's going to make me love you any more, so you never have to live to impress Daddy because you are already accepted, and that's what GOD is saying to us.

But in the body of Christ we struggle with being accepted — nobody loves me, nobody cares for me. No, what you need is a revelation that God cares for you. Nobody called me, God cares, nobody visited me, God cares, amen. Remember the Lord is checking you out, and He knows you by name, and He knows what He has destined you to be. Ephesians 1:7-11 reads *In whom we have redemption through his blood, the forgiveness of sins, according to the riches of his grace; Wherein he hath abounded toward us in all wisdom and prudence; Having made known unto us the mystery of his will, according to his good pleasure which he hath purposed in himself: That in the dispensation of the fulness of times he might gather together in one all things in Christ , both which are in heaven, and which are on earth; even in him: In whom also we have obtained an **inheritance**, being predestinated according to the purpose of him **who worketh all things after the counsel of his own will:** That we should be to the praise of his glory, who first trusted in Christ.*

✦ What is our inheritance anyway? Well, it is all that Christ is and has spiritually and naturally. In a nutshell, it is our dreams, visions and desires. But we must see them within the boundaries of God's plan and purpose for our lives. Jeremiah 29:11 (NIV) says, *For I know the plans I have for you," declares the LORD, plans to prosper you and not to harm you, plans to give you hope and a future.*

You know it does not matter when my children come unto me, my will is already made up concerning them; there is nothing that they can do that's going to change my mind on what I have for them in life, **nothing**. My will is made up; my love for them is unconditional. Who is it unconditional toward? Sons, not servants. God's love is unconditional for his children, not for his servants. And if you are trying to serve God to get his approval, you will be serving the rest of your life. But when you recognize who you are and what he wants you to become, then he will pour out on you your inheritance. God will do it; he will give it. Predestinated for sonship, so many people are trying to be everything but sons, everything but children. People are concerned about their self-worth, not realizing they are in the royal family and the richest family in the whole earth. Your Father holds the best seat, and he decrees all things; you are priceless in his sight. We struggle for lower positions, not realizing the one that God has already given. We wonder why the authority of God in our life does not manifest, the power of God doesn't manifest. We must begin to tell the earth, the devil and all the demons that we are here now (sons), and the earth should look up at us and say you sure are.

Where I live was called tornado alley about a year or two before we had our house built; one of the worst tornadoes they ever had went right through where God told us to build our house. This area used to get two to three tornadoes a year (I was told), but when we moved here five years ago we commanded the tornadoes to stop, and we have not had one since, all glory to Jesus!

God did not send you where you are to get your stuff torn up; we must stand in our positions, not as men of

God but as **SONS**. Sons change the earth realm; sons change the destiny of nature; sons move things into their proper position. Please read (Mark 4:35, Mark 6:30). This is a position that has been given to every child of God. We are all in the family; we grow up with a mind set in Christianity that only certain people get certain things, that God moves in their life that way because they are anointed.

Don't you know that the preacher goes home and has to have faith just like everybody else? The preacher (servant) needs the same revelation of sonship, and if he does not get it, he goes through just like the rest of us, amen. God is not asking the ministry gift to preach; He's commanding him. It's a part of servanthood. Paul understood this. He said, "Woe be me if I preach not the gospel and that it was better that he do it willingly, but if not willingly, a dispensation of the gospel is still committed unto me" (I Corinthians 9:16-17).

As a servant we must be obedient, but don't you know as children of God even in our disobedience there are certain things that God will do? When my children were disobedient, I still fed them. Very rarely did my children do what I told them; but I talked to them and grounded them and tried to drive the foolishness out of them (you parents know what I'm talking about). But I still put clothes on their backs, food in their bellies. Why, because they are your children, not because of what they did or did not do. God moves in your life because He is your Father. He's the God of the whole universe, but He moves in your life because He is your Father! He moves in your life because He is your Father! He knows the throne is His; what He keeps trying to reveal to us is His position concerning us, and this is the entire revelation of the new testament **sonship**. Nothing else is talked about more than this subject, and we have missed it as Christians.

✳ Christians inheritance
   dreams / visions / desires /
Supporting scripture
   Jeremiah 29:11 / Eph 3:20 / Ps. 37 / Mark 11:24

9

Sometimes my children didn't even ask for forgiveness, but what did I do? I still blessed them with those things that they needed — not wanted or desired. Sometimes I thought my children had gone crazy, or at least they did a good job of making me and their mother crazy. And what did we do? Tell them they are grounded for two weeks and let them off in two days. They make you go on a fast in the morning for their sake, and you let them go to the movie that night for your sake. Why, because they are our children, not because they did right or wrong, but because they are our children, not because they did right or wrong, but because they belong to me, amen. Don't misunderstand me; we must deal with right and wrong (sin), but we always give our children the basics, and that's what most of us as Christians have right now — the basics.

* it is more important to be an heir of god, rather a prophet or teacher because only heirs (sons) will receive the inheritance.

CHAPTER THREE

Facts and not Fiction

MATTHEW CHAPTER 16:13-14 reads, *When Jesus came into the coasts of Caesarea Philippi, he asked his disciples, saying, Whom do men say that I the Son of man am? And they said, Some say that thou art John the Baptist: some, Elias; and others, Jeremias, or one of the prophets.*

What I want you to see here is they recognized that he was a prophet or a servant of the Lord, but let's continue to read the next two verses of scripture. Verses 15-16 read, *He* (JESUS) *saith unto them, But whom say ye that I am? And Simon Peter answered and said, Thou art the Christ, the* **SON** *of the living God.*

Across the board in religion in our day right now the problem in our society is when you begin to place God Almighty the Father and Jesus on the same ground you are going to have a fight on your hands, and that's what we are doing and saying in Christianity that Jesus is the Son of God. When we begin to say that Jesus is above everything, people and religion begin to say, "No, we better cut this out right now, and Jesus is not equal with God." What that does is exclude all other religions, but we are not in a religion, we are in a relationship. Jesus being a son places him closer than anyone else could ever be and makes Jesus the only way to the Father, and Peter had this revelation.

If Jesus was just a prophet, then that would have placed him on the same ground with all the other prophets of the past, his present and his future, and the prophets would be fighting to this day who is the best prophet and which prophet do we follow. We would still be questioning who is and what is the right way, when Jesus told us himself I am the way, praise God. When Jesus stood on the ground of THE Son, he excluded all prophets. It's not that God's prophets don't exist today; it's just that they are saying what John the Baptist said, "I'm not the one, Jesus is."

Verse 17 reads, *And Jesus answered and said unto him, Blessed art thou, Simon Bar-jona: for flesh and blood hath not revealed it unto thee, but my FATHER which is in heaven.* Hebrews chapter 1: 1-2 reads, *"God, who at sundry times and in divers manners spake in time past unto the fathers by the prophets, Hath in these last days spoken unto us by his SON, whom he hath appointed HEIR of ALL things, by whom also he made the worlds.*

God did not appoint prophets (servants) to be heir, God appointed his SON to be HEIR of ALL things, which means servants don't get anything because the son has been appointed heir of all. *Verses 3-6 read, Who being the brightness of his glory, and the express image of his person, and upholding all things by the word of his power, when he had by himself purged our sins, sat down on the right hand of the Majesty on high; Being made so much Better than the angels, as he hath by IN-HERITANCE obtained a more excellent name than they. For unto which of the angels said he at any time, Thou art my SON, this day have I begotten thee? And again, I will be to him a Father, and he shall be to me a Son? And again, when he bringeth in the firstbegotten into the world, he saith, And let all the Angels worship him.*

God is trying to give us insight into the angels that what they recognize is the anointing and authority of **SONSHIP**; what the angels move according to is sonship. What the angels are wanting to see is Christ the Son of God formed on the inside of you and me. This is a mystery Christ in you, the hope of glory, Colossians 1:27.

Now I know that all of you reading this love God's word and that you are students of the Bible, so let's just read some more facts. In the book of Matthew chapter 14:22-33 are the scriptures that deal with Jesus walking on the water. Now let's pick up this narrative in verse 31 right after Peter began to sink. *And immediately Jesus stretched forth his hand, and caught him, and said unto him, O thou of little faith, wherefore didst thou doubt? And when they were come into the ship, the wind ceased. Then they that were in the ship came and worshipped him (Jesus), saying, Of a TRUTH thou art the SON OF GOD.*

Now remember that the Bible says that he has given you and me the power to become SONS. We are trying to make ourselves into everything else, a better CEO or supervisor. Those of us in the ministry try to make ourselves better pastors, or a better husband, a better wife. No, God is saying, BECOME what you are supposed to be. Just become; it is a natural out work of the life of Christ with in you if we allow the power to work. We live in a time when we can imitate so many things; we can speed things up and make it get here quicker. Not so with sons, we must go through the process of becoming. We can get imitation orange juice which is what most of us settle for, the imitation, but if you want real orange juice you have to wait for that orange to get ripe. It has to grow on the tree, and that takes a little time, but it is becoming what it's supposed to be. You can go and prophesy to that orange tree to be an apple tree, but that orange tree is going to look at you and tell you I am becoming what I'm supposed to be. I'm becoming just what I am, what I always will be, that which God has spoken to me from the foundation of the world. The orange tree does not know how to be anything else but an orange tree.

The reason a lot of us as Christians are not content with who we are right now is because we have been an imitation of something that we are not. The reason that we have been struggling with so many things in our walk and in our lives is because there is one thing and one process that will always be going forth in our lives, no matter what we try and do, and that is becoming a son. That power is working in us right now.

In the gospel of John chapter 9 the scripture talks about Jesus healing the blind man, and after he was healed he is made to tell his story to the Pharisees, the religious people of the day. After he told them, they kicked him out of the church because he said Jesus healed him. In verses 35- 37 look at the profound statements Jesus makes himself. *Jesus heard that they had cast him out; and when he had found him, he said unto him, Dost thou believe on the SON OF GOD? He answered and said, Who is he, Lord, that I might believe on him? And Jesus said IT IS HE that talketh with thee.* God the Father has said it; the disciples have decreed it; now Jesus himself is acknowledging it; I am the SON OF GOD.

Children can get things done that outsiders could never do. We think as servants we know how to get the hand of God to move. Oh, but watch what will happen if you start approaching Him as one of His own. Parents can say no to everyone else, but let our children approach us and we just give in, amen. The Bible says

If we being evil know how to give good gifts unto our children, how much more shall your Father which is in heaven give good things to them that ask him.

The key word is FATHER, which means we must approach him as SONS (family), Matthew chapter 7:11. We stand in being a Christian, but God wants us to boast in being sons. Just go ahead and make the devil mad and say, I am a son. Tell the devil, don't make me go to Daddy because if I do I'm going to tell on you. My daughter was that way; if my son did anything, she was going to tell on him. Somebody would get in trouble. And this is the way we must get with the devil. Michael told satan, satan, the LORD rebuke you.

Hebrews 1:1-2 give evidence of sonship

Acts 27:21-25 gives example of angels acting on the behalf of the sons of god

Acts 12:1-10 Peter in jail

Matthew 3:16 gives evidence of sonship causing the heavens to open (John baptizes Jesus)

⇒ <u>God responds audibly & visibly</u>

Matt. 3:16

Sonship causes the heavens to open
Explain the situation, when heard god say
this is my beloved son .. & they saw the
dove.

CHAPTER FOUR

Well Done or Well Pleased

MATTHEW CHAPTER 3:13-17 says: *Then cometh Jesus from Galilee to Jordan unto John, to be baptized of him. But John forbad him, saying, I have need to be baptized of thee, and comest thou to me? And Jesus answering said unto him, Suffer it to be so now: for thus it becometh us to fulfil all righteousness. Then he suffered him. And Jesus, when he was baptized, went up straightway out of the water: and, lo, the heavens were opened unto him, and he saw the Spirit of God descending like a dove, and lighting upon him: And lo, a voice from heaven, saying, This is my beloved Son, in whom I am well pleased.*

Now the first thing that we need to see is in verse 16 heaven opens when you approach God on the grounds of sonship. How do we know that Jesus did it on the grounds of sonship and not as a prophet? Because verse 17 tells us that the Father said, "This is my beloved son in whom I am well pleased."

We also see something else in verse 17. To servants, it's your reasonable service; you have done your duty. Some of us do it unwillingly, but if you do, God says well done. But well done does not always mean that God is pleased with you; it just means that you did your job; you got it done. But to sons God always says, I am well pleased with you, because everything that sons do

17

they do out of love and not out of service. God is not just saying, well done, you did a good job, servant. You have servants that serve unwillingly doing stuff grudgingly, but sons always do it because they love papa, and God always says, oh, I am so pleased with you. Doesn't it just bless your heart when your children do something for you just because they love you? Now you just can't help yourself; you just have to hug them and go get them some candy or something because of what they did for you out of love. It takes our children a long time to learn this lesson, to do things out of love. They think that we bless them for what they did so they do more, but a parent always knows when the child does something out of love, and when they do we can't help ourselves, it just makes us want to do something for them. This is the way God is with us. God already provides for us but when we start doing things for Him because we love Him He can't help but open the windows of heaven and pour us out a blessing, amen.

To this day most Christians serve God because it's all about what can I get from God. God knows our motives, and we don't realize that everything that belongs to God is already ours and so all that we do as sons we do because we love God; we are not trying to get anything because we have everything already. So whatever God wants us to do, we do it because we love him; no hidden agenda is involved, praise God! Sons have the revelation that God is going to bless them whether they do or don't do. Servants have the revelation that says I have to do something to get something. Servants think that their much doing pleases God, but we must understand that this is stinken thinken, because on the grounds of a servant you will never be able to please God. You will always fall short as a servant because you are trying to get something that does not belong to

18

you. The inheritance belongs to the sons (family). The servant (the mind set of a servant is one who is outside of the family hoping to serve hard enough to get something) is trying to get something that is not his. That Christian's revelation is messed up.

We live in a city of a very rich family. If I said the name, you would know them. I know people who do know this family, and they always talk about them because the children have not had to work, but they have nice cars and nice stuff. But the people that I know are upset because everything that they have they had to work for it, and everything that this family's children has was given to them. The people that I know don't think this is fair, and you have a lot of God's people that have this same attitude, that if you don't work for your blessing, then you don't deserve it. That is a Christian who has never read the story of Isaac whose name means laughter. You will laugh, too, when you realize that God wants to give it all to you, amen. When you are rich, you want to bless your children's children. You don't care if they graduated from Harvard or the city college; all you know is they are your children so you go buy them a new BMW or some other car. It doesn't even matter whatever they want because you love them and they are your children, not because they did everything so right or perfect. If your father is a billionaire, you don't have any problems going to ask him for a couple of million. Oh, brother, you are breeding laziness. No, I'm not, because sons are always about their Father's business, hallelujah.

All I'm saying is when we realize who we are we don't have any problems asking for anything, and you don't say, "You know, Dad, you should do this because I did make it out of college or because I was good yesterday." Children are not concerned with what outsiders are saying about them as long as they are being blessed. They don't care if someone calls them lazy while they drive their new car, and neither should we. All we need to know is God has accepted us, amen. God may discipline you, but He is still going to bless you. He can't help Himself because He is walking with you as a Father. Saints, I'm telling you in this last hour in which we live, the anointing of God that is resting on the body of Christ that's going to bring in the blessings that everyone has been prophesying about is the anointing of sonship. God has to place it upon us; it has to rest on us and we have to grab it because it's not going to come any other way. I'm talking about the stuff that You want; it's not coming to you except through the revelation of sonship. God can't give you what belongs to Him any other way we must recognize that we are a part of the family.

Matthew 21:33-40 says, *Hear another parable: There was a certain householder, which planted a vineyard, and hedged it round about, and digged a winepress in it, and built a tower, and let it out to husbandmen, and went into a far country: And when the time of the fruit drew near, he sent his servants to the husbandmen, that they might receive the fruits of it. And the husbandmen took his servants, and beat one, and killed another, and stoned another. Again, he sent other servants more than the first: and they did unto them likewise. But when the husbandmen saw the **SON**, they said among themselves, This is the **HEIR**; come, let us kill him, and let us seize on his **INHERITANCE**. And they caught him, and cast him out of the vineyard, and slew him.*

Now we know that the servants that the Lord is talking about here are the prophets. The scripture is clear that they were not the heir, but then God sent

His Son, and the scripture is clear that Jesus is the heir and that He has access to all of God's stuff or, as the Bible puts it, He has an inheritance. But the parable goes on to tell us that the people thought that all they had to do was kill Him and they could receive His stuff, but it is clear that they could not and did not.

Two thousand years ago people did not receive Jesus and they killed Him, and He rose from the dead according to the scripture. It is tragic that 2,000 years later people are still having a problem receiving God's only begotten SON, and I would say to you that if you are reading this book and you don't have a personal relationship with God, just receive His Son right now because it is clear that you and I must be a part of the family before God will share Himself and His stuff.

The gospel of John chapter 14:6 is clear; it says that JESUS is the way, the truth and the life: and that no man comes unto God the Father but through JESUS. So I say, let's go God's way and not reject Jesus but accept Him. The message is still the same. The love of the Father, a Father whose son gave his life for others. And because of that Father's love, whoever takes the Son gets it all. People of God, we must begin to place value on the Son of God and on sonship; we must lock in on Jesus, and if we do, God's going to give it all to you, all the other stuff that we place value on. If we would just place value on sonship, God is ready to give it all to you. All we have to do is begin to head in one direction. All of that other stuff you are thinking about and talking about is yours; God has it for you.

*Phil. 2:5-8 what mind did Jesus Christ have that we too must have -

Humble / humility
Obedient
No recognition
Sonship
mature mind
willing to serve

*Biblical figures of lower social status who became spiritual leaders
Gideon   Jesus
Peter   Joseph
moses

CHAPTER FIVE

Contrast between Son & Servant

Sons Do Serve

MALACHI CHAPTER 3:17, and Philippians chapter 2:5-7 says, *And they shall be mine, saith the LORD of hosts, in that day when I make up my jewels; and I will spare them, as a man spareth his own **son that serveth him.** Let this mind be in you, which was also in Christ Jesus: Who being in the form of God, thought it not robbery to be equal with God: But made himself of **no reputation,** and took upon him the **form of a servant,** and was made in the likeness of men.*

Jesus said, "I did not come to be **served** but to **serve.**" He also said that you who want to be the greatest, let him be servant of all. We must have the mind of Christ in this hour, and that mind is a mature mind, and that mind is a mind to serve others. Sons do serve, but servants will never be sons, but children always want to be served. Biblically speaking, sons serve but servants can never attain sonship; they will always be servants, but sons do serve. Servants look for titles, but sons look for tasks; sons are never looking for positions, they are just looking for something to do. Servants are always jockeying and struggling for positions. (I'm not against school), but servants are always trying to go to school, go to college, trying to get a better job, get more educated, all for different positions to obtain a certain status quo to receive fame and fortune we go through all of these struggles. God is saying, just be a son; it's higher than all of those things.

Paul said, "I count all of this stuff as dung; it's trash, it's useless in comparison to the excellency of the knowledge of Christ Jesus my Lord." Paul went on to say, "I will give all that stuff up that I may win Christ."

Now I am not advocating don't go to school or don't set goals. No, I'm saying that we must place more value on the anointed one and His anointing than we do anything else, amen. Some ministers today are just like Paul was before he came to know the Lord. According to Philippians chapter 3, verses 4-7, Paul said he came from the right **culture** and right race; he was from the right ethnicity, and on top of all of that he came out of a good tribe or good family or right pedigree. Not only was he a Pharisee, right denomination, right school, Harvard, but he was also trained by the best teacher of his day by the name of Gamaliel. See the book of Acts chapter 22:3 and chapter 5:34. He also spoke more than one language, and we in our day boast in all of that we walk in Christianity like we didn't have to get saved (get born again or accept Jesus as your personal Lord) or because of our upbringing you were supposed to get saved. No, and again I say no; we were all sinners and needed a savior and His name is Jesus, so now we stand in all this stuff and still don't have the anointing of God on our lives.

People of God are losing their marriages, their homes, their children, their health. They're broke, bruised and battered and as quiet as it is kept, so are some of the preachers. Why? Because we must put our faith back in God as sons (family); it is the only way. Preachers today are still doing this striving to be at a higher place in the ministry, jockeying for position, trying to rub elbows with the right people for the wrong reason. Let me say this why I am here; great men and women of God know about the anointing and they know when you are around them for their stuff instead of their anointing. It is the anointing that brings the stuff; the stuff does not bring the anointing. There is one thing on this earth that you can't get through school and wrong motives nor can you buy it, and that is the anointing of the Holy Ghost, praise God forever. In a real sense that is what we are talking about. God allows the anointing to rest on sons. And God looks at us and says to His Beloved SON, "They are still wasting time, aren't they? I wished we could go on from this; they are still patty-caking, struggling over a lower position." Congregational members say I'm not even struggling because I can never have those positions; God didn't call me. The ministry gifts have made the congregational member feel as if they are not important, so they say, "Ain't no need in me fighten for no position 'cause I can never attain. Nope, God just made me a lonely Christian, I'm nothing." But if the truth be known, everyone is struggling for a position that they think is higher, but it is really lower than where you are already.

The reality is the five-fold ministry is a position of servanthood. I'm serving right now in the process of this book, but I don't mind serving God's creation and God's people. No, I take pleasure in serving, amen, but we need to see that if I'm serving, then that places you in the position of royalty or sonship. I had to work the process to prepare this book that was cooked by the Holy Ghost in the kitchen of God, and now I am serving it to you. All you have to do is sit down and eat it; I pray that you see your position. You don't even have to fix your own food. Truly according to Galatians 4:1 you are (small L) lord of all, see Luke 22:27. In Matthew chapter 20:26-28 Jesus said that I did not come to be served but to serve. He also said those of you that would be great become a servant. In other words, it is not about being seen but serving. Most of us think leadership means drink a cup of coffee and bark out orders and be seen in some high profile position, and that's not true. Leadership is about being an example and in the sphere of influence that you have, did you use it to better the people around you, their quality of living and their standard of life? For the company is only as strong as the people in it. In other words, God is never concerned about the work He is always concerned about the state of the workman, for God knows that if the workman is right the work will take care of itself. We must ask the question: do people have peace of mind? The problem with some leaders today is they did not want the position to lead; they wanted it to be lazy or to be served. What we end up with are supervisors, managers and leaders who have a position but do not know how to lead for their motive was only to get the position. Now that they are there they don't know what to do, so their sphere of influence becomes frail and the people around them become frustrated. Biblically speaking, this person would be disqualified for leadership.

In the Bible there is a word or position called BISHOP in the Greek; it is the word (Episkopos). It means overseer, to watch over with care and concern. It also means officer in charge in a real sense; it does not mean to watch the work, it means to watch the people. In other words, if the work is going bad it is because there is something wrong with the people. The rest of the definition means to sharpen another's scope as on a rifle that they can see clearer and shoot with higher accuracy.

The Bishop is one who has insight for oversight. So

if you want the oversight but you don't have the fore-sight or insight, then you disqualify yourself for leadership.

Don't turn me off yet; there is an easy fix for this. We must begin to think about those within our house (church or work place) and those outside our house, but primarily those that are already within because they have a big part to play to those outside. As soon as you do this, ideas will begin to flow to you and to those around you. Your creative juices will begin to flow. This is settled in one scripture. Matthew 7:12 says, "Do unto others as you would have them do unto you." We call this the **GOLDEN RULE,** and as a son we must ask how would I want to be treated if I was following myself all together — VERY GOOD. The revelation that we must receive is the food that the ministry serves is the food that we need to take us into a deeper realm of sonship, and if we could see what it was for we would continue to become. And it becomes our desire as the servants of the Lord to serve our family (the body of Christ) and all of God's creation. You see on special holidays like Thanksgiving families spend time together and spread the table for each other. Families enjoy serving each other in those seasons. Well, that's the way the preachers feel at every church service; they delight in seeing their family full of God, amen. You see, when you are around family you can put your guard down while you eat and be real with each other. That's when God does his best work when we realize that I'm not a servant trying to be accepted but I'm a son around my family at Thanks giving.

★ Servants look for titles; **SONS** look for tasks. Servants get promoted based on what they do; sons receive based on who they are. Who I am is why God blesses me, not what I do, but what I have become. Servants

important
Contrast between Sons & Servants

27

are always trying to make a name, but sons are trying not to bring dishonor and shame to the family name they already have. They are not trying to bring out their own name. Sons are only trying to hold onto the name they received at birth; they love the family name which is **JESUS**.

Husbands and wives nowadays don't want to be clothed within each other; they want to prove that they are their own person, Mr. and Mrs. independent. He says, "I want a prenuptial, this is mine," and she says, "I'm not taking your last name; I'm going to keep my own name." Then you are going to keep your own problems. Now remember we are talking about GOD. But if we do service to the family name and be proud of the family name and honor the family name, oh, my brothers and sisters, God will honor you. You have fathers out here in our society that have their own business and it is successful and they have family members, son or daughter (and remember scripturally speaking sonship has no gender in it more on this later), that they want to leave that business to, and the member says, "I don't want the family business; I want to go out and prove that I can make it in this world by myself. I want to go and make my own name. I want to make it in life on my own. I'm not going to ask my father for anything."

Now we are talking about an attitude here and remember we are talking about GOD. Listen, some of us wished growing up as children that we had a father that could bless us and give us something while he's living and leave us something when he dies. What most of us that feel this way get stuck with is funeral expenses and that's okay. We love our parents but our heavenly Father has an **inheritance** for us, and for the most part I don't think we really understand this.

The book of Hebrews chapter 3:1-6 reads, *Wherefore, holy brethren, partakers of the heavenly calling, consider the Apostle and High Priest of our profession, Christ Jesus; Who was faithful to him that appointed him, as also **Moses** was faithful in all his house. For this man was counted worthy of more glory than Moses, inasmuch as he who hath **builded** the house hath more honour than the house. For every house is builded by some man; but he that built all things is God. And Moses was faithful in all his house as a **servant**, for a testimony of those things which were to be spoken after; But **Christ** as a **son over** his **own** house whose house are we, if we hold fast the confidence and the rejoicing of the hope firm unto the end.* God makes clear that Moses was a servant but Jesus was and is a Son.

★ We know that we are saved by god's grace & not by our works, what does this mean for a servant receiving staff from god?

Answer won't work, because the servants cannot inherit anything.

★ why is it possible for god to say to christian well done & he's not please?

Answer because we're acting like a servant not serving out of love.

Philippians 2:5-8
    what mind in Jesus should be in christian?

Answer humility / sonship / obedient / humble

CHAPTER SIX

Sons or Children

ISAIAH CHAPTER 9:6 reads, *For unto us a child is born, unto us a son is given: and the government shall be upon his shoulder: and his name shall be called Wonderful, Counsellor, The mighty God, The everlasting Father, The Prince of Peace.*

Now what I want you to see here is children are born but sons are given. When we are born into the family of God we are children; we have to BECOME SONS and then God gives you, when you become a son, God will give you. We must understand that sonship is a position of equality and not priority meaning you are mature enough now to handle the family affairs, but not without Father's okay. It is a position that says whatever DAD can do I can do also. We are dealing with sons and not children. Sons can do because they have their heavenly Father's mind and best interest at heart. As long as you are a child, God will never give you your inheritance. He will bless you and give you what you need to sustain you. He will treat you like a child, but He will not give you your inheritance. You want to go to the movies; here is ten dollars. No, you don't need a hundred dollars, you only need ten because you are a child. You see, if you give a child a hundred dollars when he only needs ten that child will find away to spend that money because he is a child.

The apostle Paul wrote in first Corinthians chapter

13, the chapter that most of us know as the love chapter, in verse 11 he said, *When I was a child I spake as a child, I understood as a child, I thought as a child: but when I became a man, I put away childish things.*

Paul was a child in Christ, but he grew up and became a man. You can give a child what is called a play station or sega genesis, and if you have two children the other child may not say anything, but they will look at you and walk around with their actions saying, "Where is mine?" even if it was the other child's birthday. Then you finally have to tell that child, at least some of us do. Some of us give in, but we say you are not getting anything and that child starts crying. Now I did not say babies, I said children act like this. I'm talking between the ages of six to sixteen and sometimes older than that. They will break down on you right at the stage that they thought they were maturing. This is the mirror of maturity that lets the child of God know that they are not ready for their part in the family business. We are not talking about the preacher or the five-fold ministry; we are talking about our inheritance. All of the revelation that a child has is still childhood revelation according to the apostle Paul. Even their understanding is childish. This is why Christians tussle and fight in local churches and why people have left churches over things, stuff, positions, over status. Somebody else has it, so now you have to have it. That person's understanding is childish.

First Corinthians chapter 14:20 reads, *Brethren, be not children in understanding: howbeit in malice be ye children, but in understanding be men.*

Now God will still bless you and meet your needs, but He can't give you the overflow which is your inheritance. The primary part of your inheritance is the anointing of God, and it is the anointing that brings the stuff, but a child's mind is always filled with selfish thoughts of more stuff, so the child never goes to his heavenly Father just to be in His presence, desiring to satisfy His heart. The child is only there to ask for more stuff, and God cannot trust that person with the true riches. Thank God that He is never tapped out; He always give the child what they ask for but never an abundance, and His heart is longing for some of us to grow up. I pray it is everyone who is reading this book. It is time for us to put away childish things and understand who we are.

A child that does not get his way first gets mad at the parent and then jealous and envious of their brother or sister. They say to God, "How come you have not moved in my life yet? I've been serving you for nine years. How come you have not done it for me? Now that child is going to go in the room where the other child is and say, you know what they say, "Can I play with yours?" Now, remember the toy is brand new and that child says, "No, not yet," and now we have problems. The one child is going to try and take the toy, and now they are arguing downstairs very loudly, and the parent has to come downstairs and bring pace and say, "Hey, what's going on down here?" The child says, "He won't let me play with it," and that's what we do in church, except we say they are not letting me do anything.

The toys we are talking about are positions in life and in our local churches. Even the person who may have a position if they are a child and will get tired of it and want a new toy (position), and we just go from toy to toy, thinking that this is a game. I don't want to be a deacon any more, I want to be a teacher; I don't want to be a teacher any more, I want to be the shepherd. That's all child's play, and this is not a game.

Sons never even bring themselves down into this

stuff. Sons stay in the heavenlies dealing with real issues; sons are the ones really getting things changed in the body of Christ; sons don't care if they have a title or not as long as the task at hand is being accomplished. The scribes and Pharisees which were the religious leaders of Jesus' day were always concerned with the Lord's authority or his position. While they debated over the positions, Jesus was getting people healed, delivered and blessed. He was always about His Father's business, and we have gotten so concerned about position that no real spiritual work is being done in our churches and communities.

☆ Evolutionary process of a teknon & a Huioi Child growing up into maturity. a Christian accepts Jesus as lord & Savior, So a child is born into acceptance & grows through obedience & matures to a Son of god. Christian is now in a position to be used by god because he has endured the process of becoming.

CHAPTER SEVEN

Servants, Children, or
Sons Defining Terms

THE WORD SERVANT in the new testament is only mentioned 153 times. Children in the new testament, in the Greek is the word **Teknon**; it's only mentioned 218 times. God talks about children more than He does servants. Sons in the new testament is the Greek word **Huioi**; this word is mentioned **453** times, more than servant and child put together. I would say that this is very important to God.

In the body of Christ you have a people who have an attitude of servanthood, which is good in its proper place, but if not, it will mess you up. I mean, always try to be accepted through your serving God, thinking that this pleases Him and will make Him pleased with you, but remember, only to sons does He say well pleased.

So in the new testament if you are a part of the family of God, there are really only two types of people, children or sons. You are either a teknon or a huioi, so when you see adults in the body of Christ acting like children, don't tell them to stop acting like a child. That might offend them; just tell them to stop acting like a teknon, and then they will ask you what is a teknon and you can tell them that it is a Christian acting like a child. Jesus scripturally speaking was never a teknon;

neither was he ever addressed as a teknon by his Father (GOD) but only as huioi, because Jesus always showed the dignity and character of God. He always responded with mature conduct, amen. It is not so much that you and I mature in a certain position or office as much as it is that we mature into sons.

Please allow me to be redundant for a moment and give you a few definitions. 1) HEIR — is a person who inherits or is legally entitled to inherit through the natural action of the law another's property. 2) INHERITANCE — to transfer property, or the act of inheriting ownership by virtue of birthright. 3) BIRTHRIGHT — the right that a person has because he was born in the right family, which is normally given to the first-born son. Now stay with me; that includes all of the women out there reading this book because we are talking about GOD. Using myself as an example to see what God wants us to see, I will say that I was not born into a bad family. I just was not born into the right family, because even if I was the firstborn it would not have done me any good because the only time that the birthright has any significance is if you are in a family that has something to give you. We are not just talking about good morals, even though that is very important. So it's not just about being born as much as it is being born in the right family. This is why Jesus said you must be born again, John 3:7. All Jesus was saying to us is that you need to be born into the right family. Naturally speaking, you normally do not receive your inheritance until the person who has it dies. This is why initially you receive what is called the birthright or you are firstborn. In other words, you are sealed until it's time. Now it is clear in the Bible according to Romans 8:29, Colossians 1:15 and 1:18 that Jesus Christ is the firstborn and that we are in him, which makes us all firstborn. Since we are all firstborn, then we all have a right to the inheritance, so then your birthright is vitally important. Now the birthright is what you receive at birth. You get it just for being born, not because of anything that you did. Your birth is the certificate that decrees you are the one, that all the stuff in the family's inheritance is yours. But we are born babies; we don't understand, we don't have a clue. We get a little older and become children and we still don't have a clue, but God is walking around with you from the time you are born, showing you and telling you, "You are my firstborn; all that I have is yours." The child says, "Yeah, yeah, I know, now can I go and play?" He knows but he does not understand the significance, responsibility or magnitude of what God is showing and saying.

Now God gave us the birthright story very clear in Genesis chapter 25 of Jacob and Esau. The Bible says that Esau despised his birthright; he placed no value on it, not realizing that it was the birthright that gave him the right to the inheritance. That is going on with so many Christians today because they do not understand their birthright; they miss out on their inheritance. Esau gave up his birthright sold it for one bowl of soup. He despised it, placed no value on it because he did not know who he was and what belonged to him nor the family he was born into. We are royalty; remember, he gave it all up for some soup. What will you give yours up over — fussing and fighting with your brothers and sisters in Christ, not recognizing who you are? We must understand that the child does not receive the inheritance and it is not given in that sense when someone dies but, thank God, he rose again. No, in reality it is given when somebody finally decides to grow up and become a son. As soon as we do this, our inheritance is on the way and nothing and no one can stop it. You see, Esau wanted the blessing without the responsibility of the birthright. It is the birthright that we must guard or there is no blessing; in the birthright God commands complete obedience. Isaiah 1:19 says if you be willing and obedient you shall eat the good of the land. So in Christendom we have a dilemma because we don't understand why we have not received our stuff. We know that we are children of God or that we have a birthright, but what we don't know is that we must grow up. Our heavenly Father knows when that is, and as quiet as it is kept, so do we. We ask questions like, "God, how come it has not happened for me," and His reply is, "Because you are still a child."

God is still spoon feeding a lot of us. He is saying, "I need some people to do some work around here," and while He is looking around we are still trying to get the spoon in our mouth or the bubble gum out of His pocket. Finally one day one of the children comes and tugs on Him and says, "I don't want to play any more; I am ready to work." God says, "You don't want to go back outside and play with the other children?" and that child says, "No, I just want to be around you, Dad."

Now if you don't have any children, what I am saying may not mean too much to you, but I have two. When they were young, they would often play outside all day, playing with the other kids in the neighborhood and acting like I didn't exist. I sometimes felt I was only there as a "money tree." That hurt my heart. There were times in my life that I had to make my children come in and spend time with me. Now I know that I am not the only parent who has gone through this, but think about God. When will we honestly be concerned with what is on His heart? Amen. This is the way Jesus approached everything. His heart was, "Dad, I'm not being nice because I want something; I just like being around you." "What do you want to do today?" "Father, I want you to have it your way, what will please you today, not because I have to, but because I want to."

Jesus was only one son, but what was in the bosom of the Father and what got into the heart of Jesus was an entire kingdom of sons. Jesus knew he had to die to please his Father, John 12:24-26, but it was the joy that was set before him that gave him the strength to go to the cross. The joy was he saw me and he saw you as he saw himself, a son with the ability and maturity to do the Father's will, Hebrews 12:2.

Two stories, there is a man who has a company, and he goes out of town. He started to build it and now it is an empire. While he is out of town, they have a meeting; the vice presidents are there; senior vice presidents, junior executives are there. You get the picture, and they sit around this big desk and have this big board meeting and they're all in their prestigious positions, and they begin to make decisions without the owner being there. They say, "Well, he is going to be gone for some time and we need to go ahead and do this." When they said that, one of the owner's sons just walks into the room, and they look at him like what is he doing here. The son was not on the board, and he was not one of the presidents or a junior executive; he was not invited to the meeting. He was not supposed to intrude on their meeting. Their attitude was one that said, "Don't you know who we are?" and when he walked in, silence seemed to enter with him. You know how it is when you enter a room sometimes. So he asked the question, "What is going on?" and they said, "Nothing that you need to concern yourself with." He said, "I know that I am not on the board of this company. I just came to see what my dad was up to, and they said simultaneously, "Dad's not here," so he said, "Then what are you all doing?" They said, "You are not on the board, but we are making decisions to do this that and the other," and the son said, "I don't think my father would want you to do that." And they said, "Who do you think you are?" and he replied, "I am His SON. They said, "We don't see your name on anything," and he said, "My name is not on anything, but I am His son, and if you make this decision without him I will tell him to fire all of you."

It is not being in a certain clique or a certain position, congregation or denomination. That is not what we are talking about. Sons have the ability to hire and fire people; they don't have to be a part of some company, but they must be part of the family. Blood is thicker than, well, you get the point.

Ford started a company, the auto guy, he started the assembly line. His thought was we can make more cars for less if we can get this process started; he was one of the big brains behind the operation. When he started giving out stock to buy into the company, people (one family in particular) thought they could buy enough stock and thought they had enough clout to buy in and take over. Millions of dollars were being thrown around. Ford said, "Wait a minute, I am not giving this company to any of you." They said, "We helped you with your ideals and your creativity; we are the ones who helped you and taught you how to make this company; we deserve something." But Ford said, "Yes, but it is my company and I have the right to do with it what I want. I have some sons (now at this time his sons had not shown up one day for work), and I am giving this company to them. After all of their labor and ingenuity, all of their effort and long hours, Ford told them,

"You can't have any of this company; it's mine and I am giving it to my sons." Now this is a true story. Do you know who he was talking to — a family by the name of Dodge. They left and started their own company. And Dodge did the same thing; they left the inheritance to their sons. This is how it works. Ford and Dodge used to be together, but Ford was large and in charge. Biblically speaking, Dodge was servant to Ford, and servants only receive wages but not the inheritance, only sons do.

People of God, all I'm saying is you are a part of the family and God is not giving your stuff to anybody but you. All we have to do is **BECOME.** Don't despise your birthright; be thankful for where you are right now and understand your position in the family and decide in your heart that I am going to grow up because God has something great in store for me. By the way, in the new testament servants and children are placed in the same category, Galatians 4:1 . More on this in a later chapter.

Caterpillar becomes a butterfly

In struggles we become just like the caterpillar struggling to become a butterfly. The caterpillar's change take place out ward (seen as a butterfly) while the believer's change is inward. Heart changes for believer's /sons

CHAPTER EIGHT

What Category Are You In

THE WORD BECOME in the Greek is the word
Ginomai. It means: To cause to be, to come into being,
to change or grow, to be as specified. I like that to be as
specified, to develop progressively into, to be attractive
in appearance. Example (caterpillar to BUTTERFLY).
(Let us not forget that we are dealing with GOD and
God is dealing with our hearts, the internal structure.
We have all met people who look okay on the outside
but inside they don't look so good. Well, that's what we
are talking about here), to be suitable to the dignity,
situation or responsibility of conduct that becomes. In
other words, you have progressively developed as
specified, suitably into the dignity and appearance and
able to conduct yourself responsibly in any situation
that is not only attractive to people but even draws the
approval of God Himself. This is what it means to
BECOME!

Let us also remember that when we are dealing with
sons in the scripture it has no gender to it, meaning
the word son is neither male nor female; it has to do
with maturity. There may be a job or position open right
now in your life, something that you think you can
handle, but if God does not think you are suitable,
meaning you don't fit, then that door will close. So what
happens is we end up making a lot of lateral moves in

our life or sometimes even a move down and then back up to where we where before. Now I'm talking about those of us that have surrendered our lives to God. When these things begin to happen, we begin to blame the devil or other people, but we must begin to understand that promotion comes from the LORD, Psalms 75:6-7. What God is saying is that you are not suitable because whatever God has for you no man can stop it. He (GOD) is at that time telling you and I to grow.

When I was in the Air Force, we had a phrase called conduct that becomes an officer. This was normally said when an officer got in some kind of trouble. Meaning the conduct of an officer or someone in leadership was suppose to be higher than that of an enlisted person, and rightfully so. This is why God's laws and the laws of our land are for everyone, but those in leadership must lead by example or they lose the respect of those following. What we end up with is lawlessness. No longer is God accepting do as I say but not as I do; that day is over.

So likewise, you and I must begin to have conduct that becomes sons, and if our conduct is not the conduct of sonship, then we are walking outside of our rank and delay our inheritance, because God has given all of His family a high ranking office of royalty, and our conduct must fit the office. We must remember according to Ephesians 1:6 and Romans 12:1 that God loves you and accepts you in His family, but He does not accept everything that you do. We dealt with this earlier, also that sons do because they love, but servants do because it is duty.

Philippians 2:1-3 reads *If there be therefore any consolation in Christ, if any comfort of love, if any fellowship of the Spirit, if any bowels and mercies, Fulfil ye my joy, that ye be likeminded, having the same love, be-*

ing of one accord, of one mind. *Let nothing be done through strife or vainglory; but in lowliness of mind let each esteem other better than themselves.*

The average child never exalts the other child; they must be taught this. They are always in what we call competition. This even exists in our churches. Even in the ministry people who have a call of God on their lives and a common goal to edify the church find themselves in competition. Who can out-preach or out-teach? Who has the biggest church, who is on radio or TV?

The apostle Paul would say, "Brothers, these things ought not be," amen. The misconception is we think that because God has called one into ministry that we have arrived at what the scripture calls sonship, and that's not true. It does mean that one has been gifted and graced to build, but it does not mean that you have been commissioned to do so. More on this in a later chapter.

The Bible lets us know in Romans 11:29 that the gifts and the callings of God are without repentance. If we have leaders that still act like children and have no authority over their heads, where does that leave our congregations? We are talking about sonship. One of the things that God is restoring right now in the body of Christ is apostolic authority which deals with the order of first things and accountability. You can always see a person who is maturing because when you get blessed and rejoice, that mature person will always rejoice with you. It is time for us to get glad when something good happens for someone else. If we don't, we hinder no one's blessings but our own.

Philippians 2:4 reads, *Look not every man on his own things, but every man also on the things of others.*

Lock in with me now because we said that sonship is higher than servanthood. Philippians chapter 2:5-7 reads, *Let this mind be in you, which was also in Christ*

*Jesus: Who, being in the form of God thought it not robbery to be equal with God: But made himself of **no reputation** and took upon him the **form of a servant**, and was made in the likeness of men.* Jesus did not try to make a name for himself, no reputation. We think that ministry is a step up, when really it is a step down. Because Jesus was a son who chose to serve, he took a step down; he humbled himself to serve. When ministry should have been a step down into humility, people have used leadership as a step up into pride, God's heart was and still is for ministry to be an office of humility, and where there is humility there is also great honor. Read first Samuel 9:6. We should only do what we do because it is what our Father wants us to do. Then and only then is He pleased with me and you.

In the home a child finally turns one; before that the parents had to do everything. By one the child is walking; by age two or three the child is putting on his shoes, but the shoes are on the wrong foot, shoes are untied, might be in diapers; ages four, five, and six, it's fun to help Mom and Dad. But they mess up more than they clean up, more in the way than anything, but we allow them to do because they are excited and we know that they are learning. But they are still children and to them this is fun and that lasts for a few years, okay, a few months. Now they are ten or eleven, and now house work is mandatory (some of you men are saying right now, I never had to do that stuff. Yeah, and you think your wife is your mother and she is not). Shame on the parent that does not let the child help in the home, because if you don't they won't grow up. It is called maturity, and maturity only comes by taking responsibility; it does not come any other way. When children become teenagers, they like to do things, i.e., go play. Now before they can, taking out the trash is mandatory, and my children somehow forgot to take that trash out. The reason they didn't was because of lack of obedience, when you do things out of your own free will. When it is fun and there is no mandate on you, you can stop when you want to, but as parents because we want the child to mature, they must run into authority. This is something that our society does not want to deal with because we don't want any accountability, which is what comes with taking responsibility. At ten it's fun; at fifteen it's your responsibility. Tuesday you forget; Thursday you forget; Saturday you want to go play and we have to ground you, not because we want to, but to teach you. This cycle goes on throughout life. God is telling us to do and because He is telling us to do now we don't want to do.

Marriage is the same way; you start out cooking for that man, and as long as he does not ask you to cook you're okay, but if he asks you, he just stepped over the line. All of a sudden he is telling you and you feel like a slave; your job starts out as fun, but then you are held accountable on your job, and now because you are accountable it's not fun any more. This is why people just live together but don't get married; they are running from accountability and responsibility, but what they don't understand is they never come to the place of maturity. It is something about that paper that is just too binding.

The second we rebel against God and shrug your responsibility which would have kept you on the road to maturity, you are going to deal with the Holy Spirit, and that's no fun. It's the Jonah principle. Everybody knows Jonah; he got swallowed by the whale. It's called meeting authority; your life becomes miserable until you take action and say, "Okay, I will do it." Then God lets you out of the whale's mouth and says, "Go do it." That is what the parent is trying to do with that child who forgets three days in a row to take the trash out.

In all our lives there are things that we desire to do which really was God's desire for us to do. We start and then stop, and God tells us, "No, continue," and now it's a mandate so we don't want to do. When will we learn that we don't win?

My daughter played the saxophone for many years. Now we knew that music was in her, but we never forced her to play an instrument. She came to us and asked to play. We said okay, along with almost $1500; the first year she was fine. But then she had an idea that she did not want to play any more, and I emphasize play because an instrument is not play, it is discipline, but we told her that she was not going to quit. She went silent for a day or two and then snapped out of it, and went on to be first chair in band, which is the best. That made her happy, and she did not even remember wanting to sop, but we did.

The point is, God will not let you quit. We think He does, but He does not. There is a parent out there who would say you were hard on your daughter. No, the word "prosper" in the Bible means to go forward, not backward.

CHAPTER NINE

Growing Up

AS WE WERE SAYING in the last chapter, in all of our lives we must take responsibility which brings us into maturity, and the second we rebel against that we get in trouble.

Speaking from my own life, some of you will understand this. When God called me into the ministry, I ran for over a year. I did not want to have anything to do with preaching or teaching I was content with just being a Christian, giving my tithes and saying amen and being a witness, seeing souls saved — that made my day, but God would not leave me alone (smile). But you have people who get into ministry as an occupation or just a job that pays the bills, or they think that it is fun and exciting and get over into vainglory because they think it makes them the center of attention. They really don't understand the mandate and the responsibility that God is giving them, ministering life unto His people, II Corinthians 3:1-6. This is something that you have to do if God called you to it for the rest of your life. When you don't want to and when you do, it is the same way on your jobs. You don't just show up when you want to; they will fire you. Well, in the ministry you do it even if there is no money. I said you better know that God called you to this because it is a walk of faith, so you don't do this for the glitter and glamour.

You do it because there is a mandate on your life from your heavenly Father.

People get married and the puppy love stage fades out and true marriage sets in. Then there is a scriptural command from God to treat each other right. Now it's not fun any more; it is called maturity. How do marriages last? It is called maturity. Somebody, if not both bodies, had to grow up. It is also called reciprocity, which means the law of exchange which means giving and receiving. Remember, children just insist on their way and take, take, take. That will not work in marriage. God said we must show due benevolence. Every problem in a marriage is because someone is still acting like a child. Now remember that you wanted that position called marriagehood. You saw your friends do it, your brothers and sisters do it, so you said, "I guess it is my turn." Now you have problems because someone is acting like a child. Everything in our lives as a child of God has something to do with responsibility, and you do it because you want to please God and not because you want to be seen by someone else.

So as a preacher when I go into the sanctuary and there is only one person I am still going to preach, not because there is only one person, but because that is what God wants me to do. If there are a thousand people, the answer is still the same, not to be seen but to serve. We must walk by faith and not by sight if we are doing what God has told us to do, no matter how it looks. You are successful because you are in the will of God. We must see the difference; some things that we see as tragic are really triumphant in the eyes of God because He wanted to see our obedience in a thing. It is only tragic if we choose not to do what the Lord has told us to do. Other wise you are victorious, and never let anyone tell you different, not even yourself.

CHAPTER TEN

Honour

(SERVANTS LOOK FOR TITLES, sons look for tasks.) Servants get promoted based on what they do; sons receive based on who they are. Servants are always trying to make a name; sons just don't want to bring shame to the name they already have, and the family name that we have received is JESUS.

Proverbs chapter 22:1 reads, *A good name is rather to be chosen than great riches, and loving favour rather than silver and gold.* John chapter 5:43-44 reads, *I am come in my Father's name and ye receive me not: if another shall come in his own name, him ye will receive. How can ye believe, which receive honour one of another, and seek not the honour that cometh from God only?*

It is a scary thing when we as people get wrapped up in our own name. We do it in ministries, and in marriage. Don't get mad with me. I am not mad with you. I am only endeavoring to share the heart of God with his creation and His people. I go to a church and the name of the church is your name (denominational name). Remember, biblically speaking, names mean something; they give insight into the person. This is why when you get into denominationalism, if it does not have your name on the door you won't go. Remember that the apostle Paul said that is babyhood Christianity and breeds division in the body of Christ. Please

What's in a name   honor / character

(insight into the person)

Know this

read I Corinthians chapter 1:10-17 and I Corinthians chapter 3:1-7.

It's one thing for people to tell you you were great, but it's another thing when the Holy Spirit says, "I am pleased with what happened." You know this and hear this in your spirit in your gut. Then there are other times that people will pat you on the back and tell you everything was fine, but there is no confirmation of that from the Holy Ghost, and you go home grieved all down in your gut. You just don't feel good; you are burdened and you know that whatever you were doing on that day that God was not pleased with you, no matter what people say. You may hide behind a smile in front of people, but you know you are in trouble with God. And what that causes the child of God to do is go home and say, "Father, I repent, I'm sorry," and you grow and learn from that experience. It is called being led by the Spirit and under the Lordship of Christ. On the other hand, there could have been times when the people were mad with you, but you know Dad was glad with you. Read Acts 4:19, Acts 5:29,32.

Sons attain a thing; children only see a thing, they never attain what they see. Children are always grasping for it, but it is always right outside of their reach. The reason that it is that way is because that person is a child. Now we must remember God never dangles something in front of us if He did not want us to attain it. He would not let you see it if He did not want you to attain it. But God will not allow you to attain until you come to a place called maturity. It belongs to you, but you can't have it until you grow up.

Hebrews chapter 2:9-10 reads, *But we see Jesus, who was made a little lower than the angels for the **suffering** of death, crowned with glory and **honour**; that he by the grace of God should taste death for every man.*

Sons attain + children see.

It is better because Now you know you're matured

52

For it became him, for whom are all things, and by whom are all things, in bringing many **SONS** *unto glory, to make the captain of their salvation perfect through* **sufferings.**

Hebrews chapter 5:8 reads, *Though He (JESUS) were a SON, yet learned He obedience by the things which He* **suffered.**

So then we as children of God come into sons of God by things that we suffer if we learn from it. Anytime we are disobedient to God, now I am not talking about persecution which is the wrong that you receive for the right or way you believe. I'm not talking about that. We say things like, "God, if you get me out of this I will not do this again." That is the suffering we are talking about here. We say, "I have learned my lesson, God." It could be in the area of having a heated discussion with your spouse — because Christians don't argue, we have heated discussions — or it could be in a place of a wrong financial decision. We say, "God, get me out of this situation and I won't do it any more. Two years go by and you do it again.

Now let me share a revelation with you. Obedience cannot be taught, but it must be learned. Don't misunderstand me; we can go into the classroom and teach you the biblical principles about obedience. We can show you godly examples of obedient people in the Bible, but that's not where you learn it. Let me say again, obedience cannot be taught from the pulpit, but it must be learned. Jesus was a man who knew everything, but He had to learn one thing and that was total obedience to the Father to walk in heaven's power. Read John 4:29, and Luke 4:1. If Jesus had to be led by the Spirit, how much more do we need to be led by the Spirit of God? It is when we don't allow the Spirit to lead us that we suffer. It was not because He did not try to lead us; it

Being led by the spirit is Obedience of honor

53

is because we refused to listen. The Holy Spirit said inside of you, "Don't say that to your wife or husband," but you say it and I did, too, and we suffer, amen, but we learn to listen, praise God. Then after we have learned the lesson we try and help our brothers and sisters, and we say don't go there. They say, "Why?" and we say, "Just don't go there," but what do they do? They go there and learn a hard lesson. There are two ways of learning, by mentor or mistake. One is the lowest and slowest form of teaching. I'll let you decide which one it is for yourself.

Children, because they are children, will never say I was wrong even when they are wrong and know they are wrong spiritualize and scriptualize and scripturalize everything to smooth over and justify their actions, but sons have enough humility to come back to that person or mentor and say, "You were right, I missed it. I should have listed to you."

Hebrews chapter 2:11-12 reads, *For both he that sanctifieth and they who are sanctified are all of one; for which cause he is not **ashamed** to call them **brethren,** saying, I will declare thy name unto my **brethren,** in the midst of the church will I sing praise unto Thee.*

Jesus is calling us His brothers. Hebrews chapter 12:5 reads, *And ye have forgotten the exhortation which speaketh unto you as unto **children,** My **SON,** despise not thou the chastening of the LORD, nor **faint** when thou art **rebuked** of Him.*

It is amazing to me that when a message comes forth that we don't like too much we get upset. As long as the shepherd is preaching a (bless me) message, we are okay and the shepherd is great and anointed. But if he preaches a correction and instruction message or talks about sin at all or repentance, we go home mad, don't show up for two weeks, swear he was talking about you, not realizing that the message is for the whole church, and then wonder why things aren't going well. It is because we all must grow up and allow GOD to speak in his own House. Remember, don't despise the chastised and don't faint. Sons can take it because they know that through this we grow.

Hebrews chapter 12:6 reads, *For whom the LORD loveth He chasteneth, and scourgeth every **son** whom HE **receiveth**. Remember unto us a child is born, unto us a son is given,* Isaiah 9:6.

God accepts children, but He does not receive them into His bosom. No, children are kept under tutors and governors until the time appointed of the Father, Galatians 4:2 (we will develop this in a later chapter).

Everyone that is not a son, God does not allow them to rest in His bosom; He keeps them at a distance. Otherwise they will see and hear things too early and not have the spiritual strength to hold it. We talk about enduring things all the time, but God said in Hebrews chapter 12:7, *If ye endure chastening* (the spanking of the Lord), *God dealeth with you as with **sons**; for what son is he whom the father chasteneth not?*

We like the atta-boys and the pats on the back, but as soon as a ministry gift (church leader) walks up on you and says you have been messing up, even the way you were acting in church today is not going to make it. As soon as that happens, grown people will pouch their lips out and begin to pout. If God has to correct us through the servant of God or by the WORD of God, we get an attitude. We must endure the chastening of God, for how we receive it decrees if we are sons or children. Sons endure it; children don't, and this measurement will let us all see where we are. Spiritually speaking, we all know how we act when a certain Word comes forth in God's house. We like instructions, but we don't like correction.

According to the book of II Timothy 3:16 and Isaiah 28:9, God does not give us instruction unless we receive correction first. He gives no knowledge unless we are off the breast. We must mature before God will really begin to talk to you vertically. Your destiny is wrapped up in how you and I receive correction because our course is never given in detail unless we receive the correction. Believe me, when I tell you our destiny is straight and narrow but very, very possible and very blessed. You may see it, but you will never understand how to attain it, which is the performing of a thing without the sovereign discipline of the Holy Spirit.

Hebrews chapter 12:8 reads, *But if ye be **without** chastisement, whereof **all** are **partakers**, then are ye **bastards**,* (illegitimate or without a Father) *and not **sons**.*

God is saying, "I don't even claim you as mine if you can't endure chastisement." Now remember we are talking about sons and not children. I pray that what I am about to say helps some families out. In western civilization divorce is at an all-time high, and that's not a good statistic. The point I'm making is not the divorce, but the children. Whose are they in the sight of God, speaking from a father's prospective? You see most of the time you have one man who runs away (normally the paternal man), and then you have another man who comes in and marries, and he prays and stays. The question is, who is the father? First, you are not a father because you got someone pregnant. A true father is the man who stays and takes responsibility for the children in his care. Does he love, nourish, provide, protect, chastise and correct? If he does those things, then he is the father. Just ask the wife who has a good man or a child who has a good man over them if they feel like a second wife or a stepchild. They will say, "No, I feel like the first wife and an only child because he treats us special." If this is true, then why don't we give him his rightful title of Father, which is what he deserves, which simply means this is a man who takes responsibility for another person's welfare and actions. A child is not a bastard because he does not know who his paternal parent is; a child is a bastard when they refuse correction from the parents that are with them every day, and this is what God is saying to you and me. If we don't want to go His way, then we are on our own.

Hebrews chapter 12:9-11 reads, *Furthermore we have had fathers of our flesh which corrected us, and we gave them reverence: shall we not much rather be in subjection unto the Father of spirits, and live? For they verily for a few days chastened us after their own plea sure; but He for our profit, that we might be partakers of His holiness. Now no chastening for the present seemeth to be joyous, but grievous: nevertheless afterward it yieldeth the peaceable fruit of righteousness unto them which are exercised* (trained) *thereby.*

Now I know that God's position on this subject is not popular in our society, but we must remember that God has not changed even though we have. Society has taught us to just be passive in our position as parents, but what that breeds in our children is a life that is out of control, undisciplined, irreverent and not responsible. Parents tell me all the time, "I don't know what to do with my children; they don't listen to me. They are out of control." God's answer to that is they have not been trained. Don't say amen yet; most adult Christians don't take responsibility either, because they refuse to be chastised or corrected (trained). Please read Hebrews 12:12-24.

My children, when they were young, thought that because they were good that I would bless them more, or because they did something right that I was going to do something more for them. Now that is what people do, but that is the wrong way to raise children. A child gets a C, we give them $5; B, $10; A, $20. That's the wrong way the child should get good grades. Because you teach them, train them and tell them to, the child should do right because you tell them to. So now in our society everything is based upon a pat on the back. No pat, no work, and that does not work in adulthood, even though that is the way most adults are today. Even in our churches no one is doing just because God said so. Why are you doing what you are doing? Because God told me to. People don't believe that when you tell them that; they think that there is something behind it. That is what we have made Christianity — an attaboy society, meaning you live for God because He is going to do something for you. Well, God does do things for us, but not on those grounds. This is why so many churchgoers have stopped going to church, because they were taught an attaboy gospel. You do this and God will do this, and that gospel is not completely true.

Now you have been with me this far, don't unlock now, just hear me out. Most of us don't do things simply because God told us to or because it is the right thing to do. We do it because someone is watching, and if we don't get a pat on the back we are prone to stop. In our day we are okay with someone receiving an award as long as we are that someone. If we are not, we get jealous. In this hour God is checking the motives of our hearts, and sons do because God said so and because they love God. The gift of God and the blessing of God is not released because of our praying prophesying, or fasting. It is predicated on a fact are you a child or a son. For a lot of us it is not that our prayer was wrong; it's the ground from which we are praying that disqualifies us for that which we prayed for. See James 4:3.

It is not that God does not want you to have, it's just that you are not mature enough or you are not able to take responsibility for what you are desiring. So my children had to learn that they have to do what I tell them to do because I tell you to and I am not playing all the games with you. They had to learn that I do for them because I love them, not because of an A on a report card. I had to teach them that they should do for me because they love me because love is always obedient. The highest level of love is obedience. This is why when a person tells me they love God but they don't do what He says, I know they don't love Him. Now I know what you are saying, you are saying (Don't tell me I don't love God). I John chapter 5:2-3 reads, *By this we know that we love the children of God, when we love God, and **keep His commandments**. For this is the love of God, that we **keep His commandments:** and His commandments are not grievous.*

I John chapter 3:22 says, *And whatsoever we ask, we receive of him, because we keep **His commandments,** and **do** those things that are pleasing in **His** sight.*

We must remember that true love, God's love, agape love, is unconditional love. Marriages would be stronger and last longer if we understood real love.

I John chapter 3:1-3 reads, *Behold, what manner of love the Father hath bestowed upon us, that we should be called the **sons** of God: therefore the world knoweth us not, because it knew Him not. Beloved, now are we the **sons** of God, and it doth not yet appear what we* *shall be: but we know that, when He shall appear, we shall be like Him; for we shall see Him as He is. And every man that hath this hope in Him **purifieth** himself, even as He is **pure.***

① Sons are honored by god, god gives them
Authority / wealth / increase
a good name in the earth
Positions of trust & authority

The two sons demonstrated being lost

Sermon topic: "from Son to Servant"
(are you a son or servant?)

✧ CHAPTER ELEVEN ✧

Two Sons

LUKE 15:11-32 IS THE STORY about the prodigal son and his older brother, and it reads as follows. *11) A certain man had two sons: 12) And the younger of them said to his father, Father, give me the portion of goods that falleth to me. And he divided unto them his living. 13) And not many days after the younger son gathered all together, and took his journey into a far country, and there wasted his substance with riotous living. 14) And when he had spent all, there arose a mighty famine in that land; and he began to be in want. 15) And he went and joined himself to a citizen of that country; and he sent him into his fields to feed swine. 16) And he would fain have filled his belly with the husks that the swine did eat: and no man gave unto him. 17) And **when he came to himself,** he said, How many **hired servants** of my father's have bread enough and to spare, and I perish with hunger! 18) I will arise and go to my father, and will say unto him, Father, I have sinned against heaven, and before thee, 19) And am no more worthy to be called thy son: make me as one of thy hired servants. 20) And he arose, and came to his father. But when he was yet a great way off, his father saw him, and had compassion, and ran, and fell on his neck, and kissed him. 21) And the son said unto him, Father, I have sinned against heaven, and in thy sight, and am no more* *worthy to be called thy son. 22) But the father said to his servants, Bring forth the best robe, and put it on him; and put a ring on his hand, and shoes on his feet: 23) And bring hither the fatted calf, and kill it; and let us eat, and be merry: 24) For this my son was dead, and is alive again; he was lost, and is found. And they began to be merry. 25)* **Now his elder son was in the field:** *and as he came and drew nigh to the house, he heard musick and dancing. 26) And he called one of the servants, and asked what these things meant. 27) And he said unto him, Thy brother is come; and thy father hath killed the fatted calf, because he hath received him safe and sound. 28) And he was angry, and would not go in: therefore came his father out, and intreated him. 29) And he answering said to his father,* **Lo, these many years do I serve thee,** *neither transgressed I at any time thy commandment: and yet thou never gavest me a kid, that I might make merry with my friends: 30)* **But as soon as this thy son was come,** *which hath devoured thy living with harlots, thou hast killed for him the fatted calf. 31)* **And he** *(the Father)* **said unto him, Son,** *thou art ever with me, and all that I have is thine. 32) It was meet that we should make merry, and be glad: for this thy brother was dead, and is alive again; and was lost, and is found.*

First we must understand that this is a story about two sons that were lost. One left the house and one was in the house; one left and became lost because he did not want to obey his father's rules and take his responsibility. The other stayed and became lost because he was in legalism of the law, but in the covenant of grace everything happens by faith which works by love, and what they both missed was the father's LOVE.

Now let us go deeper into this from the scriptures themselves. In verse 12 the younger son asked for his portion, but the father did not give him his portion. He gave them out of his own, not what belonged to them. God never gives us what is rightfully ours until we are ready for it. Though he was a son, he was acting like a child. Let us not miss the terminology that Jesus is using in this story — **Father, Field, Son and Servant**.

Now we know that the younger son was acting like a child because he asked to leave and because verse 13 tells us he wasted his money and that's what children do all the time. It is not wrong to spend money, but the Bible is clear what he spent it on, carefree living or riotous living, not responsible. Verse 14 tells us that he spent it all and was in want. The Bible tells us that the Lord is my shepherd and I shall not want. Any time we don't want to go God's way we end up in need. Verses 15 and 16 tell us that he had to go into the field. Representing a servant or your own strength, you are in a rut instead of being in a groove; nothing is running smooth. The husk represents yesterday's garbage, what the people did not want to eat. That word husk means just the shell like a peanut shell without the peanut, which means he was not satisfied and could not be satisfied where he was. It means that he was just a shell of his former self, that he is yesterday's news. One day you are the star of the football team; the next day you are a nobody. He felt alone; no one gave to him.

I believe a lot of people go through this and are still going through this emptiness of life and purpose. This always happens when we get out ahead of God and out of His plan for our lives. People ask, how do you slow things down? You must pray. The type of environment the younger son was in, God uses it for His good. It is His desire according to verse 17 that we will **come to ourselves** and remember that we need God in our lives and start thinking about going home in our day.

That means, get your heart right and then find yourself a good church. Pray and ask God to help you do so. This is what happened to Naomi in the book of Ruth 1:21. She said, "I left home full, but I have come home empty."

Please listen to his mindset in verse 17. Sin has warped his thinking; he understands that God is still his Father, but he has lost his identity in being a son. He left home a son, but he came home with a servant's mindset because his memory was of his older brother and his father's servants. To him they were all one and the same, but from his viewpoint at that time even this was better than where he was at because he was perishing. But he still does not see from the father's view point.

I would just like to say here that older brothers need to do right, because younger family members are looking at you. In God's house we must remember that God does not give inheritance to servants, only to sons. He will provide for you, but He won't give you your own, and so many of us still have not learned this. We are still trying to work our way in to get God's approval. As quiet as it is kept, a lot of family members are trying to do this with their own parents, still not understanding that their parents love them just the way they are. In God's eyes, Jesus does not care if you are a judge or a janitor. He just wants you to be pure and mature in your heart. According to verse 18, our level of turnaround is predicated upon our understanding of whom we have hurt. It is good to forgive yourself; it's good to tell a wife, husband, brother, or friend that you have done wrong. But until we realize that we have hurt our Father, then full deliverance never comes forth because people have the power to forgive but not the power to cleanse and deliver. Only God can do that, and remember, to repent just means to have a change of mind. We can speak it, but God is the one that gives us the strength to do it, amen.

Let us also remember that we don't repent just because we don't want to get in trouble, but also because someone has been hurt in the process, meaning repentance is not just about you.

Listen to his speech in verse 19. Now he is still just thinking this it has not happened yet, and he says I am not worthy to be called thy **son:** make me one of thy hired servants. He is trying to work his debt off his sin. He wants to be a servant. The elder brother served to obtain the father's love; the younger brother was going to serve to obtain his father's forgiveness, and both of them are wrong. Verse 20 says he went home and the father saw him from a distance. Oh, we need to understand that as soon as we begin to take steps toward repentance God comes running to us. Before we can even get our prayer out, God is there wrapping around us arms of love. He had compassion which is love in action. Oh, parents could learn a good lesson from God. When children want to leave (18 and above and out of high school), help them leave. If they leave wrong, love is what brings them back, not us running out there after them, but when they come we must love. The only way they will come is when they come to themselves. Remember in the bible that a kiss always has to do with relationship, and fellowship it means to revive, restore and recover. How many of us need that. It means what is mine is yours, and God has a lot.

Verses 21 and 22, listen to the son and the father's speech. Though he wanted to be a servant, he grew up and became a son. How do we know? Because he took **responsibility** for his own actions. See, when the father saw him, he did not see a child or a servant; he saw a son. He knew it was one of his from a distance. The son's experience had formed and fashioned him into a son. It matured him; he took responsibility for his actions, and most people in our society don't but sons do, but he says in verse 21, "Father, I am not worthy to be **called** thy **son**." But the Father ignored him and spoke to his servants. A lot of times God ignores us because our approach is wrong, and he said to the servants, "Bring the best robe," which stands for **royalty**. He felt unworthy, but the father said he was royalty, so many people have such low self-esteem you just need God to talk to you for a few days, that's all. Then he put a ring on his finger which represents **authority**. Isn't it funny how royalty and authority go together — not his own authority, but his father's authority. God is bringing him into full sonship. Now he did not give him the ring when he left the first time because he was not ready, but now wherever he goes people must do because of the ring. You see, it is not by power or by might but by God's spirit; promotion comes from the Lord. The father put shoes on his feet, which represents **triumphant**, that the devil is under your feet, that there is no weapon that is formed against you, that shall prosper, that there is no enemy that can stop the plan of God for your life, that there may be people out there who don't like you, but they cannot stop you, praise God forever. I am preaching myself happy!

Verses 23 and 24 — the father killed the fatted calf which represents a sin offering. After we repent there should always be rejoicing, reconciliation and restitution. We must thank God for Jesus before and after becoming Christians because we know that even after we become Christians we sin and make mistakes, but first John 1:9 says that if we confess our sins He is faithful and just to forgive us of our sins and cleanse us from all unrighteousness. Verse 24 says he was dead and lost. To be away from God is to be dead and lost, but to come home means to be alive and found what a great feeling to feel alive.

A lot of people are just existing, but they don't understand that Jesus came that we might have life and have it more abundantly. What a wonderful thing not to just live life but to **have** life. Verse 25 says that the elder son was in the field working. After all these years he is still acting like a servant, hoping his father will take note of him. So many people in the body of Christ are just like this, trying to work their way into a blessing, not realizing that the blessings of God cannot be worked for but must be inherited and received by faith. Verses 25-28 say the elder brother heard music and dancing inside the father's house. This lets us know that there should be a sound of rejoicing in our churches, but the son questioned it. The servants told him that his brother had come home and the father was having a celebration because of it. And the Bible says he was angry and would not go in. Let's see why? Verses 28-29 say his father came out and asked him what is going on, and the elder son said, "These many years do I **serve** thee."

You have many a Christian just like this who gives tithes and offerings, active in church and never receives anything from God. Why, because the revelation is not based in what you do but in who you are, and this son was in the right house but he only had the revelation of a servant. Neither transgressed I at any time thy commandment, and yet you never gave me anything. Do you see that his faith was in his own self righteousness? He was legalistic; he walked in the letter of the word and not in the spirit of the word of grace and the gift of God which comes to us by grace. Grace cannot be earned, and so many Christians still have not learned this. They go through life with calluses on their hands, never coming into the full blessings of God for their life.

Don't misunderstand me, I am not talking about using grace as a license to sin; I am saying use grace not to sin, that we never come before God in our own merit. The Bible says that our own righteousness is as filthy rags, and so many people still have not learned this lesson and message of faith.

Now listen to what he says in verse 29. He calls himself a servant, and in verse 30 he calls his little brother a splurger and a womanizer, but he also called him a **SON**. I wanted my children to go to college and make an honest living, but if I neglected to tell them about God and how to walk by faith, they would grow up thinking that it was their own effort that got them where they were. We all need to understand that without God where would we be. Any of us could have been on drugs and without a job, living on the street. Oh, I'm sorry many of us were that way but God came into our lives, so instead of pointing fingers we need to be thanking God that we are not. But because we don't understand our position, we become arrogant and prideful, when the scripture admonishes us all not to put our faith in things, stuff and money, but it never said that we could not have it, just not to trust it. So when he compared himself to his brother, which is never a wise thing to do, he basically said, "I am better than him." Yet he also said, "Even though I am better, I still have not received what I feel I deserve," and this is because God is always looking at us on the grounds of sonship which deals with growing up which always includes our faith **IN GOD** and not in self.

The Bible is clear that only faith pleases God. Now

look at what the father said to him in verses 31 and 32. Let us remember that the elder son expresses how he feels to the father, but listen to what the father says. That day brought two sons home; one went the legal way, the other went the rebellious way, but they both had to come the mature way. The father said, "**SON**, you are ever with me, it's not the work I'm looking at. It is you I want, and **ALL** that I have is YOURS. The Bible says you have not because you ask not. All he needed to do was ask, but he didn't. He stayed out in the field, and the only thing that brought him in was the music. One son did nothing but work, and the other son refused to work, when all he wanted from both of them was their love or themselves. It is you that God wants.

Even in our homes husbands miss this a lot of times. It is not enough for you to go to work and equate that for the totality of love, when that wife and those children need you more than they need your money, and you think that because you are the CEO of a company that they should be happy. But they are not. To them that man is MIA, because they want him and not just his money. When we walk in love, we understand verse 32. We should be glad when a family member finally comes home with a right heart and a right mind because the younger son did not just come home; he repented; he changed; he grew up, amen.

⟡ what was each son in the Prodigal son parble trying to gain

    their father's love

     acceptance

     approval & affirmation

CHAPTER TWELVE

Receiving Him

LET US GO BACK to our original scripture text for a moment. We have covered so many things, but let us see something else in this verse of John 1:12. It says as many as **received him** to them that received him, gave he power to become the **sons** of God. Let us understand that the them is anyone. Anyone can receive him, so this has nothing to do with ethnicity, education or economics. God is no respecter of persons (Acts 10:34). Let us remember that you can only become what God has destined and ordained you to be; that is where you will find true joy and peace. And what we have all been destined to be are sons of the Most High God.

Let us remember the caterpillar; you may be a caterpillar today, but you are going to fly tomorrow. We must remember that there is a higher calling than an apostle, and it is to be seated with Christ as sons, Ephesians 2:1-6, Philippians 3:13-14. We must stop fighting over positions below us and as sons willingly by the will of God step down into them to bring people up to Him. God wants all of us to be sons. It would be tragic if it was only for a few, but it's not; it is for all. No matter what anyone would say to make us believe different, it's not true. God wants me and you to be sons, praise the Lord forever! You may not be a preacher, a teacher or a deacon, but you can be a son, and if you arrive at sonship there is an inheritance for you.

Philippians 2:5-8 says that Jesus was obedient unto

death, even the shameful death of the cross. First Samuel chapter 15:22-23 reads, *And Samuel said* (to Saul the king), *Hath the LORD as great delight in burnt offerings and sacrifices, as in **obeying** the voice of the LORD? Behold, to **obey** is better than sacrifice, and to hearken than the fat of rams. For rebellion is as the sin of witchcraft, and stubbornness is as iniquity and idolatry. Because thou hast rejected the word of the LORD, He hath also rejected thee from being king.*

The thing that we need to understand about sons is that they obey. Children stray, but sons obey. We can always ask ourselves one question: Have I truly been doing what my Father has been telling me to do? If you believe that you are doing what God is telling you to do, then you are coming into maturity, but if you are messing around, then you are a teknon and you are not going to come into your inheritance that way.

I have two children, and my son is the oldest. There were things around our home that were his responsibility as a teenager. Let me just say this here that some of us need to get off the bottle, and I am not talking about alcohol; I'm talking about the baby bottle. There are three stages in our Christian walk: babies, children and sons. The more responsibility you take decrees what stage you make it to. So my son had responsibility in our home. One of them was to cut the grass. He was supposed to do that once a week. Two weeks would go by, still no grass was cut, three weeks went by. Now the grass was between my shin and my knee. I didn't say a thing; fourth week comes, still not cut. Now I have to say something. "Antwone, how come you have not cut the grass?" The first week it may not look too bad, but the fourth week the grass begins to talk to you, and it says, don't you think I need a trim? So I know that if Antwone forgot that after the fourth week the grass itself would remind him. You see, he is my son, but he is acting like a child, so I go to him. "How come you have not cut the grass?"

Now remember Samuel chapter 15 that says to obey is better than sacrifices. The sacrifice is your apology. No, I am tired of your apology. Just obey. Too many people have worn out "I am sorry." God is through with it. So now what the child will do is cut the grass and clean the room. This is their sacrifice to get back into your good graces. But God has already told us earlier that we are already **IN HIS GOOD GRACE,** that we have already been accepted, so I cannot accept my son any more than I already have. I already love him because he belongs to me, and sacrificing does not change how I feel about him because my love as God's is is unconditional. There is nothing that he can do that will make me love him any more. So if Tiffany brought home an F or an A on her report card, I still love her. But if he did not cut the grass or if she brought home an F, they were going to have to pay the piper because I love them dearly.

Discipline and correction must come forth now. To obey and listen is better than the sacrifice. In other words, do what God tells you to do the first time. That scripture goes on to say that rebellion is as the sin of witchcraft. Now if I were to stand up and say that we have some witches in the church, people would be trying to stone me, but God said to not do what He said to do is as the sin of witchcraft. You will not do what He said do and choose to be in control of your own life; no one can tell you anything. This is what is wrong with our churches today; people don't want to listen to their mentor, priest or clergy people, change churches like they change from McDonald's to Burger King, all because they don't want anyone to speak into their hearts.

This saddens the heart of God because He knows that true character and growth only happen in the home, which is the local church that you and I attend. Ephesians chapter four.

So my son finally cuts the grass on the fourth Saturday. Do you know what I say to him? "Well done, you finally did it. He is acting like a child. I do not say well pleased because I'm not pleased. Three more weeks go by and he has been consistent cutting the grass every week without me telling him, so now we are on the fourth week again. I go somewhere that morning and come back, and he is outside cutting the grass and I did not have to say anything, so my speech changes and I say that I am well pleased. Do you know what this does in my heart to see him out there handling his business. If you are a parent, you know the feeling that I am talking about, but let us remember that we are talking about GOD. This does something in the Father's heart when He sees you doing something without Him having to tell you three times to do it. Now you are starting to walk in sonship; now you are doing it because you know that it pleases Him and not because He told you to do it. Now He will begin to bring you into His bosom and share more. Do we do things out of duty or out of love? Are we servants or sons? I want God to be pleased with me; I don't want Him to say, well, it is about time you did it, whatever (it) is only you know.

You can always tell a man that does not cook in his own house because if he does it once in that calendar year he makes a big deal out of it. He asks the children how was it; he asks the dog can you smell it, and then he is waiting for his wife to comment on it. What you want her to say is you did a good job, and if she doesn't you are going to have a fit. You see, you want her to say well done, but she knows that this was a one-time good deal, something that she does every day. If you really want her to change her attitude and her speech, do it more often, and she will say well pleased. That won't be the only thing cooking that night. Well, God is the same way, amen.

You can always see the maturing children of the Father because they don't make a big deal when they do something because they are always doing what pleases the Father. Let us remember according to Hebrews 12:23 that we are all firstborn, which means that you and I have a right to the inheritance of God which is normally reserved for the oldest son. Thank God for Jesus. In God's family there are no elder children; there is only one child, and his name is Jesus. We are in Him, so we are all firstborn so we get to appropriate, and participate, in His inheritance. God has enough in Himself to bless the whole world, and we would still just be in the first one percent of all that He is. First John 3:2 and 4:17 read, *Beloved, now are we the sons of God, and it doth not yet appear what we shall be: but we know that, when He shall appear, we shall be like Him; for we shall see Him as **He Is**. Herein is our love made perfect, that we may have boldness in the day of judgment: because as **He Is,** so are we in this world.*

The thought that must get out of our thinking is that God only has something for us in the sweet bye and bye. Now that is true, but it is not the complete truth. The rest of the story, as Paul Harvey would say, is that God has something in store for us while we are here on planet earth. The reason that Christians lose their faith and stop serving God with fervency is because after they give their life to Jesus they don't know what to do, and that's because we develop a concept that puts all blessings in the future somewhere, specifically heaven. Well, if Jesus delays His coming for just three more months, you will be discouraged because you think that the only thing God has in store for you is heaven, and that is not true. God has something in store for you now. Faith is always in the present tense. God wants to bless you now! The blessings of God are only predicated on one thing — growing up, going from children to sons because only sons receive the inheritance, so there is a mandate on all of us to grow up in the grace and in the knowledge of our Lord Jesus Christ. If we don't, your Father and my Father will withhold our inheritance. You don't need a title to lay your hands on the sick; all you have to be is a son. "This is my beloved son in whom I am well pleased."

Please remember Luke 15:25-32 about the elder brother of the prodigal son, that he thought to work harder would make his father happy. He never had the revelation of who he was. The younger son came to himself. He realized who he was, and when he came home his father received him as a son and not as a servant, and the father blessed him. But the older brother was angry because his **brother** was being **blessed.** How many times have we seen this in our churches — envy and jealousy. All of that is immaturity and lack of understanding of who you are. In the body of Christ no longer will God let us get away with acting like babies. If you are saved, you understand what I mean when I say that the Holy Spirit will jump all on your back for that because we know better. In verse 29 he said he served and received nothing. In verse 30 he said that his younger brother was a son and his father blessed him, and in verse 31 the father called the elder brother Son and said all that I have is yours. The revelation is one of sonship, and if we don't see this, though it all belongs to you, you won't receive any of it. All you will get is a servant's reward. That's okay, but it is not the inheritance. In Matthew 17:5 it reads, *While he yet spake, behold, a bright cloud overshadowed them: and behold a voice out of the cloud, which said, This is my beloved Son, in whom I am well pleased;* **hear ye Him.** Children are born but sons are given, Isaiah 9:6. John 3:16. This is the scene at the mount of transfiguration. The two other people that were there with Jesus were Moses and Elijah. But the Father said, "Listen to my Son; hear Him. Moses represents the law and Elijah represents the old testament prophets, but Jesus is the Son of the Living God." So the voice of the hour that really has power in it is the voice that is coming out of the maturing children of the Father. There are a lot of people speaking that have names and titles, but their words don't have the (oomph) to help get you through life; only the voice of the son can do that. I will go further to say that apostleship was ushered in with sonship, so true authority comes from one being a son (mature), Hebrews 1:1-2.

Please remember that I am not being critical of anything or anyone. I am only sharing what the Holy Spirit has released me to share. Titles mean nothing without maturity in the person that has it. Mature ministry comes from having a mature person in it. In Matthew 25:19-21 is the parable about the talents. In this parable we find out that servants receive based on what they do. Some people see God as their creator, others as savior, some as Lord and some as Father. How you see Him decrees how you will live before Him. When you start seeing Him as Lord, you are one step away from sonship, but so many people stop right there and have an attitude that says I must do something to get something. But if that person does and does not get, they will stop serving God, or to them Christianity becomes a form of slavery and legalistic. Jesus is LORD, but we need both revelations and keep all four steps in their chronological order, that God is creator, savior, LORD and Father. If we mess this up, we get into trouble because God will exercise His Lordship over us any time He wants to. People want God to be their savior, but they don't want Him to be their Lord. In other words, tell them what to do after they get saved, and if we don't allow Him to be LORD, we will never know Him as Father.

The point that I am making is, if you approach God as a servant, your attitude will be if I do something for God He better do something for me. What have you done for me lately is our cry, and if He does not move soon, we will stop serving. This is a wrong attitude because sons do serve no matter what God does. Rewards based on what one does is the way of the world, but it is not the way of the kingdom of God. Lordship in His eyes is you do because I told you to. That's Lordship, not Fatherhood. You see, servanthood, stewardship and faithfulness are all just one door, but that door leads one into sonship, Galatians 4:1, first Corinthians 4:2, Luke 16:12. Most people go to God for God to do something for them, but very few go to God that they can do something for Him. Sons endeavor to please their Heavenly Father, and this has even been lost in our natural society. Most children could care less if their parents are pleased with them or not. This open conflict started back in the late fifties and early sixties and continues on here in the late nineties. Someone must stand in the gap and make up the hedge; someone has to be a repairer of the breach and a restorer of paths to walk on. Especially since we live in a society where government and educators are trying to tell us that 12-year-olds have rights, and they do but not the way it is being legislated. The child doesn't work, won't keep their room clean, the computer that they use belongs to the parents, the clothes that they wear the parent bought; the food they eat, the bed that they sleep in — all come from the parent, but we say that the child has rights and build in them a false sense of security because that is not real life. Everywhere in society there are rules and laws that we must all abide by, and what we are building in our children is if they don't like it, just rebel.

Let that child get in trouble; they are going to blame the parent and hold the parent responsible. Let's just hope that whatever the child did did not hurt anyone or cost any money, or the parent is going to be held accountable for that, too. Our public schools make decisions concerning our children that the parent knows nothing about until after the fact. They call and tell us what they are going to do instead of calling us to ask us what we want to do. Legislators instantly break down all levels of authority when you remove the parent from their position to raise their child the best they know how. I am convinced that 95% of all parents genuinely care about the best interest of the child that they assisted God in bringing into this world. I say with all boldness: give us back our children. We live in the hour where the hearts of the fathers are being turned back to their children, and the hearts of the children are being turned back to their fathers. See Malachi 4:5-6, Exodus 20:12, Matthew 15:4-6, Matthew 19:19, Ephesians 6:1-3.

We have a misconception that God can't make it without us, but the truth is we can't make it without Him. It is in Him that we live, move and have our being, so it is with our children. Parents don't center their lives around the children; the children are supposed to center their lives around their parents. This is where the child's true freedom comes from, to be loved by their parents, hallelujah. Most of our children only hang around us when they want something, but what a joy when they start hanging around you even when they don't want anything.

In God, life is not about what can you do for me; it's what can I do for you. This one thought can save a lot of marriages if we work it out practically in everyday life.

I Sam. 15:22-23 benchmark for becoming

Deal with principle of obedience

Christian cannot become without doing what god said he must do.

3 from the hall of faith
(how did their faith pleased god)

Abraham
Noah
Enoch

CHAPTER THIRTEEN

Faith To Please

MATTHEW 3:17, ROMANS 1:17, Hebrews 10:38-39, Hebrews 11:5-6, John 8:29, Hebrews 12:2 say this:

*And lo, a voice from heaven, saying, This is my be-loved Son, in whom I am well **pleased**. For therein is the righteousness of God revealed from faith to faith: as it is written, THE JUST SHALL LIVE BY FAITH. Now the just shall live by faith: but if any man draw back, MY SOUL shall have no **pleasure** in him. But we are not of them who draw back unto perdition; but of them that believe to the saving of the soul. By faith Enoch was translated that he should not see death; and was not found, because God had translated him: for before his translation he had this testimony, that he **pleased** God. But without faith it is impossible to **please** Him: for he that cometh to God must believe that He Is, and that He Is a rewarder of them that diligently seek Him. And He that sent me is with me: the Father hath not left me alone; for I do always those things that **please** Him. **Looking unto Jesus the author and finisher of our faith**; who for the joy that was set be-fore him endured the cross, despising the shame, and is set down at the right hand of the throne of God.*

The Heavenly Father says to sons, "Well pleased," so we know that Jesus, the Son of God, walked by faith because you can't please God without it. We must understand that only the maturing children of the Father (sons) are really walking by what the Bible calls faith. Faith is what causes you to truly be obedient unto God, because anything that God tells you to do is going to take faith to do it. It takes faith to love, it takes faith to forgive. Children walk by their senses, what they see, but sons walk by faith. The reason so many Christians don't obey God is because you can only see God by faith. Most of us only trust our own ability and resources, and because we can't see it in ourselves we limit God also and come to the conclusion that whatever it is it's impossible, Luke 18:27.

Matthew 17:19-20, Mark 9:23 reads, *And He* (Jesus) *said, the things which are impossible with men are **Possible** with God. Then came the disciples to Jesus apart, and said, Why could not we cast him* (the demon) *out? And Jesus said unto them, Because of your **unbelief:** for verily I say unto you, If ye have **faith** as a grain of mustard seed, ye shall say unto this mountain, remove hence to yonder place; and it shall remove; and nothing shall be **impossible** unto you. Jesus said unto him, If thou canst **believe,** all things are **possible** to him that **believeth).***

This type of thinking is easily fixed by getting out of our traditions and opinions and getting back into the Word of God. Mark 7:13 and Proverbs 3:5-7 says, *Making the Word of God of none effect through your traditions. Trust in the LORD with all thine heart; and lean not unto thine own understanding (opinion). In all thy ways acknowledge Him, and He shall direct thy paths. Be not wise in thine own eyes: fear the LORD, and depart from evil.*

This is why some scientists and biologists have problems believing that God made the world we live in. Because the way they gather facts is through the senses or by what they find or see.

I don't fault them for that, so they choose to believe that out of chaos came order. But the Bible is clear that it takes faith to understand that there was a planning, thinking God who created this world. Please read Hebrews 11:1, Genesis 1:1, John 1:1-3, Hebrews 1:10, Romans 8:24-25, II Corinthians 4:18, Hebrews 11:3.

*Now **faith** is the substance of things hoped for, the **evidence** of things **not seen**. In the beginning God created the heaven and the earth. In the beginning was the Word, and the Word was with God, and the Word was God, The same was in the beginning with God. All things were made by Him; and without Him was not any thing made that was made. And, THOU, LORD, IN THE BEGINNING HAST LAID THE FOUNDATION OF THE EARTH; AND THE HEAVENS ARE THE WORKS OF THINE HANDS. For we are saved by hope: but hope that is **seen** is not hope: for what a man **seeth**, why doth he yet hope for? But if we hope for that we **see not**, then do we with patience wait for it. While we look **not** at the things which are **seen**, but at the things which are **not seen**: for the things which are seen are temporal;* (changing and changeable) *but the things which are **not seen are eternal**. **Through faith we understand that the worlds were framed by the word of God, so that things which are seen were NOT made of things which DO APPEAR.***

Faith is the ability to walk out on nothing and step on something. Faith is the ability to walk to the end of this world and step into God's world. Trust is the ability to have faith in someone else to intervene in your life. Sons live by faith; it is their lifestyle. Faith is the force that lives in the Father that only functions by love and fixes all fractures and strengthens all frailties that He touches. God is the only being that has a right to

Author define Faith
Know

83

put Faith in Himself. The rest of us are encouraged to put our faith in Him.

Mark 11:22 says *Have Faith in GOD.* Faith produces the fruit of humility and dependency upon God. Your revelation of God determines your worship; your worship determines your obedience; your obedience determines your maturity, and your maturity decrees your faith. The more mature you are, the more dependent one becomes, totally trusting in God. Simply put, what you see by the eyes of faith is going to determine what you become, or how mature you will be in Christ.

I Corinthians 2:9-16 and Hebrews 11:27 says, *But as it is written, Eye hath not seen, nor ear heard,* (that is the natural eye and the natural ear) *neither have entered into the heart of man, the things which God hath prepared for them that love Him. But God hath revealed them unto us by His Spirit: for the Spirit searcheth all things, yea, the deep things of God. For what man knoweth the things of a man, save the spirit of man which is in him? Even so the things of God knoweth no man, but the Spirit of God. Now we have received, not the spirit of the world, but the spirit which is of God; that we might know the things that are **freely given to us of God.** Which things also we speak, not in the words which man's wisdom teacheth, but which the Holy Ghost teacheth; comparing spiritual things with spiritual. But the **natural man receiveth not the things of the Spirit of God:** for they are foolishness unto him: **neither can he know them, because they are spiritually discerned.** But he that is spiritual (mature in God) judgeth all things, yet he himself is judged of no man. For who hath known the mind of the Lord, that he may instruct Him? But we have the mind of Christ. By **FAITH** he (Moses) forsook Egypt, not fearing the wrath of the king: for he **endured,** as **seeing** Him who is in-*

visible.

This is an oxymoron. How can you see God since He is invisible? Only through the eyes of faith, praise God forever, amen.

Most people have an intellectual faith, meaning they only mentally ascent to God, head faith but not heart faith. You see, the Bible is clear that you have to believe with your heart and not your head. So many people fall short of real Bible faith, meaning the scriptures are good until it applies to them. Once it applies to them, they might hear it but they won't do it. God is real as long as He does not mess with them or their traditions. True bible faith is to act on the scriptures you know or have knowledge of. If you believe it, you will act on it or do what it says to do. We must not only be hearers of the Word but doers also. Otherwise you are not walking by faith, and you are walking in what is called self deception. See James 1:22-25.

You see, God has no problem being our Father; we have a problem being His sons, and until we settle this issue that God is God and that's just the way it is, we will never come into the fullness of what He has for you and me. That is, spirit, soul and body, naturally, physically and materially. If we would be honest with ourselves for a moment, most of us are not where we would desire to be, and all of our strength and ingenuity is not going to get us there. God is saying, "Come, just come home. I have a good plan for your life." See Jeremiah 29:11-13.

Children think they're in control, but sons know they're not. The more you know God, the more you realize that you are not in control of anything. It's called true humility and brokeness; that's what faith is. When you hold a baby in your arms or the hand of a dying loved one, you realize that you are not in control, and at that moment you feel little or you abase yourself. God said when you do that He exalts you and raises you up. That feeling should be in us every day that God is in control. This is the ground that you see the miraculous of God, that nothing is impossible with Him! When we arrive at this place, we find out that there is nothing that God can't do, and it brings a state of peace, trust and rest over our lives to know that you are in God's hands. This was the ground that Enoch walked on, and he was not, for God took him. When you and I walk by faith, people don't know where you are. They can't find you; you are to far out there, but God and the others walking by faith know where you are because they are out there with you. I believe that those of you reading this book are not of them that draw back off what God has said to you that we don't draw back off of what we have said to God. We are those that hold fast to our confession to the end; we are those that believe that our dreams and visions come to pass, amen. So many people say I want to please God, and God is saying the only way to please Him is to walk by faith.

Sons have a heart to forgive even before the person says I am sorry. Jesus said forgive them because they know not what they do. The disciples asked Jesus a question how many times should I forgive my brother, seven times? Jesus said, No, until seven times 70, which is 490, and that's in one day, meaning in your eyes it never happened. The disciples said, "Lord, increase our **faith**" (Matthew 18:21-22 and Luke 17:1-5).

I can hear you husbands and wives saying the same thing. I can even hear some of my brothers and sisters who left local churches wrong, saying it also. Let us remember that unforgiveness in one's heart is a sign of immaturity, and to truly forgive takes faith. Why do we want to grow up? So that we can receive our inheritance, and it's not just you wanting it; your heavenly Father wants to give it. Daddy is not trying to withhold anything from you, but He understands that He cannot give you things that you are not ready for. We would not allow our children to drive without a license, would we? So we don't give them our car just because they think they can drive. No, we give them the car after they prove they can drive and receive their licenses. For me personally, even after my son received his license, he might have met the state requirement but he did not meet mine because when he drove I was still nervous in the service. Some of you know what I am talking about if you had to help with the teaching aspect of your child's driving. It was better me than my wife; I just don't know if she could have taken it. I mean, we are talking about **walking by faith.** Thank God we made it out okay. You don't start a child out cooking steak; you start him out boiling water. For some people they can't do that; they will burn water if you let them.

All I am saying is God wants you to have it more than you want it, but He only gives to those who are ready.

⚐ *Christians* approach god from the
DO perspective instead of the Be perspective
tithing serving & worshipping pg# 67

→ The demon's ignore the disciples commands
because of lack of faith & unbelief in Jesus
& their own authority

⊗ Faith & trust is the ability to walk out on nothing & step on something (faith) ability to have faith in some one else to intervene in your life (trust)

CHAPTER FOURTEEN

Maturity Is Found in Intimacy

WE MUST ARRIVE at a place of maturity which is the place of intimacy. In the Bible this place is called Abba. Abba in the scripture is in the vocative voice, meaning that Abba is a personal name of God or only applies to God. Whereas father is not a name as much as it is a position or place that one holds in the family (people may call me apostle, but apostle is not my name; it is my vocation and position in the church). But Abba is like a pet name for God, but only family is allowed to use it and not just family but close family, because it is the place of intimacy.

For example, my children are not allowed to call me by the pet name that my wife calls me by. I only respond to it if my wife calls me by it and no one else. My wife's and my pet name for each other is Babe. My children's pet names are pooh pooh man and tinka lady, and only my wife and I are allowed to call them this. And they respond to it when it comes from Mom and Dad. For anyone else to say it would almost be sin. Today you have people in families, they are so formal with each other, this is only because they have not reached the place of intimacy. It scares me when I hear a husband and wife always call each other by their first name, and it saddens me when I hear children call their parents by their first name. To me it is a sign of not just distance but disrespect, because Mom and Dad will always be Mom and Dad, no matter how old we as their children get.

Well, God is no different. The pet name or intimate name that He responds to was given to us by Jesus, and He was in the bosom of the Father. This name is deeper than just Father; this is the name that God responds to when you are close to Him, and that name is Abba or Pappa or Daddy. It is very informal and intimate, and most people cannot see themselves calling God Daddy. Oh, but that is the relationship that He wants with all of His children. To know God as God places you in His hand, to know God as Father places you in the right home or family, but to know God as Abba places you in His heart, it is called delighting yourself in the Lord.

David was a man that was after God's own heart. Remember, children are born but sons are given. Sons are those who know the Father's heart and discern the intimacy that is flowing from the Holy Ghost to call God something else other than what you normally call Him. At first you don't know what it is, but it has been in the scripture all the time, Abba. It is more of a spiritual feeling of intimacy rather than actually calling out the name, even though calling out the name in that place would be appropriate. Even David had a pet name for God; it was a poetic name for JEHOVAH called JAH. Jehovah was the Jewish national name for God, but the sacred, secret, silent name for those who were intimate with Him like David was Jah. See psalm 68:4-6.

Most of the names for God in the old testament either describe what God has done or who He is, and we learn a lot about Him. It is like talking to someone all day, and then you realize that you don't even know their name. This happened to Jacob after he spent a night with God, and God changed his name to Israel. Then he in turn asked God what is your name. He did not ask him, "Are you God?" He knew it was God. No, he asked what is your name because he experienced something intimate with God, an intimacy that will make you ask what is your name, and God has told us through Christ when it is. See Genesis 32:22-32.

When you get close to someone, you want to know their name. It is sad that some people have never even asked God His name. The mark of sonship is this word Abba or intimacy with God Almighty. This word is only used three times in the scriptures, all in the new testament. Every time the word Abba is used it is always dealing with or connected with sonship. Sonship must be reached in order to use this wonderful name of God. Out of all of the names of God I believe that this one (other than the name of JESUS) is the most important because it has to do with you positionally in His Family. Sonship is always implied when the name Abba is used. God does not use Abba in general terminology. All throughout the new testament the Holy Spirit only deals with this name when He wants to make specific points, and the specific point that God wants us to understand is that Abba is only in the vocabulary of sons. Some people may call me Mr. Sanders, others Apostle Sanders, someone closer might call me Cornelius or Neil for short, but only my children call me Daddy. That's it, just Daddy or Dad. How to hear it stirs my heart and arrests my attention. Oh, the thought gives me joy. Sons are those who walk real close with God that don't just want His hand, but see His face and desire His heart. They don't want just relationship but fellowship and communion with God; they don't just want His

P Abba is only used 3 times in the scriptures all in New Testament

stuff, they want Him. Sons are worshippers. Most people are praisers at heart, which means they only praise God or thank God if He does something for them. If God does not, they will not praise God, but a worshipper is one who praises God and thanks God, not just for what He done but for who He is. So even if He does not do anything miraculous in my life today, I can still praise Him for who **He is,** and my Father is seeking true worshippers. I pray that you are one. I cannot begin to tell you how much your heavenly Father loves you. The real question is, do we love Him?

The first time this word Abba was used is when Jesus was at Gethsemane or the place of pressing. When the press is on is when we find out if we are children or sons. Mark 14:36 reads, *And He* (Jesus) (the son of God) *said,* **Abba,** *Father, all things are possible unto thee; take away this cup from me:* **nevertheless not what I will, but what thou wilt.**

Jesus' prayer was for the Father's heart to be satisfied. The second time this is used is in Romans 8:14-15, and it reads, *For as many as are* **led** *by the Spirit of God,* **they are the sons of God.** *For ye have not received the spirit of bondage again to fear; but ye have received the Spirit of adoption, whereby we cry, Abba, Father.*

Before I give you the third time it is used, let me give you two more definitions that are very important. The first word is **Adoption**. I am going to give you our basic English definition, and I am going to give you the Bible definition so that you and I understand fully what God means by this word adoption. The definition that we know is that a married couple or a person goes to what we call an adoption agency, and at first they are going to check us out to make sure that we are all right, but after that you go in and pick a child that you think suits you. I am not making light of this; I am just being basic, that out of all of the little children that were there you chose a certain child. That alone should make that child feel special. Now that is the English definition, and that is enough to shout and rejoice that out of all the people on the earth that God chooses you to be a part of His family. To this day I still don't understand why He chose me, but He did and I for one am very thankful, so every child of God needs to know that they are special and never doubt it again; God chose you.

Now that is only a partial definition of what the scriptural meaning of adoption is. The rest means this: the word **Adoption** in the new testament from the Greek is the word **Huiothesia.** Now we learned earlier that the word child is teknon, and the word for son is huioi. Now the word adoption does not mean teknonthesia; it only means Huiothesia. So then when God adopts, He does not adopt children, so this lets us know that this is something that happens after we are in the family, so the question is not are we in the family. The question is, has God huiothesia you, adopted you? God only adopts sons; He does not adopt children. We must understand that we are His children. If we have received His SON Jesus Christ, but then He has to receive us or adopt us, so when God comes into the room of His own adoption agency which is the local church, what He is looking for are sons. He is asking the question, are there any sons in the house? He says, I want a son, and He picks one out of all of those children that are already His. They belong to Him, and He goes in there and looks for one, and He says you are the one. You look like me; you are acting like me; you are talking like me. Yes, out of all your brothers and sisters you are the one; I want you by my side.

Now how does this happen? This is not respect of person or favoritism. He can only adopt you if you have chosen to grow up. The rest of this definition literally means this: remember that it is a compound word of **HUIOI AND TITHEMI** and it means placement. It means the son who has been placed or the placing as a Son.

The closest thing that we have to this in our day that most people would be familiar with would be Prince Charles and his family in Europe; he has a couple of children. Now Prince Charles, if everything goes okay and he stays the way that he should, he will be **HEIR** to the throne. Now, biblically speaking and even over there to some degree, this definition of adoption is brought out.

Just stay with me a little bit longer. Now remember, children are born sons are given when we are born into the family. According to John 1:12 it says as many as received Him, but if you read Hebrews 12:6 it says that if we endure chastisement that **He receives us as sons.** You see, children receive Him, but He does not receive them; He only receives sons, mature ones. As a child, God says you are a part of the family. Now what you go into is correction and instruction. God begins to instruct you through tutors and governors, he does not do it Himself; He places you into someone else's care to learn about Him. This is done by the Holy Spirit and the ministry gifts listed in Ephesians 4:11. All the tutors and governors for most of you is your local shepherd, so you must make it past them before you get to Him. Many Christians are flunking God's spiritual boot camp in the local church, and somehow we think that we can bypass this adoption agency, and we can't. All the tutors and governors are teaching you is how to please your Father so God brings you into the family, but He does not even allow you to hang out with Him. Some of you might call this boarding school. He gives you to someone else to train you and raise you up, but these tutors and governors have been commissioned to do this. He puts you in their care. Now it becomes their responsibility at that time until you come into sonship and Dad adopts you back and says you are ready, not ready to leave the local church, but ready for personal time with Him and the fullness of your inheritance. He keeps you in with tutors and governors, and they don't want to know what you like; they are there to teach you what He likes and what He wants. So children are taught things like this, where does Dad like to sit, he likes to sit at the head of the table; what does Dad like to drink, Pepsi; is Dad left-handed or right-handed, right-handed; where does he like his spoon, on the left side; what is his favorite color, blue. So the child begins to learn everything that his father likes, what business is Pappa in, the business of people. So we must learn the family business; we must learn Daddy's ways, we must learn what He likes and what he does not like, so that when we come to the adoption agency part of our lives what God is looking for are people that **KNOW HIM**. He is looking for people that know how to and want to please Him. You are the one that begins to say, "No, no, Dad does not like his spoon on the right side; he likes his spoon on the left side. Only sons respond this way.

If a child was to pull out a yellow suit, the son would come up and say, "Daddy does not like yellow, he likes blue." Well, I want to do this and I want to do that. Yeah, but the business that Daddy is in is the business of people. You see it is not about us; **it is all about Him.** We must begin to see that every and anything that we do in life ties into the family business; there is not a vision that God gives that does not somehow pertain to His purpose. I want to do this or I want to do that. Well, you are not ready to be a son because sons only live to please their Father. It becomes their whole purpose in life; their cry is not my will, but thy will be done. We cannot be **heir and joint heir** until we learn this lesson. Jesus learned obedience by the things that He suffered. This is why we cannot despise our birthright.

Prince Charles is Prince Charles because he is not able to be King Charles yet. But if Prince Charles was to be like Esau which the Bible calls a profane person because he despised his birthright and that word profane in the Bible means to cross the line or step over to show irreverence, Prince Charles could lose his heirship to the throne and his inheritance. You see, it is in his reach, but he does not have it yet, and a lot of us as people of God don't have ours yet either. So while he is prince he still has to do those things that please the throne, and so do we or we can disqualify ourselves for the inheritance. This is a lesson we must learn and a test we must pass.

When God adopts us, what He is saying is you are the one who is ready to please Me. Just bringing this back around to where we can understand this, how many of us as husbands and wives truly live to please each other. I mean, husband, if you have two cars, your wife should be driving the best one. If we only have one car, I guess that means that the husband is going to buy himself a bicycle. Why? Because we are living to please each other. If the husband does not like lemonade and only likes grape koolaid, there should always be some in the house for him. I can remember when we were in Japan and my mother came to visit and she was about to cook some vegetables, but they were a kind that I don't like. My wife did not stop her from cooking them; she just started making some that I do like. My mother said, "Why are you making those?" and she said, "Because my husband does not like the kind that you are making." You see, the difference is my wife had come to know me. Even though this was my mother, you don't know how good it made me feel on the inside for my wife to do that. Your husband likes his steak medium well and you bring it medium raw and tell him to be happy you cooked something. You see, you don't get up under God's skin like that because He will not even let you that close to Him until you grow up.

Husbands and wives should pretty much know each other like clock work. You see, the Bible says that God is the Lord and He changes not. You can count on Him to be the same tomorrow as He is today. That is called security and stability or someone you can count on and depend on or just simply trust. If God liked it yesterday, guess what He will like it today. If He did not like it today, He won't like it tomorrow. What I am saying is God our Father is easy to get along with. He is not scizzo nor does He have multiple personalities, and He won't deal with you until you get rid of your double-mindedness or as long as we halt in between two opinions. He allows those tutors and governors to deal with all of that carnal stuff. We must live to please, and we must live to give our lives to God completely.

Some people would say, "I don't feel close to God." Well, the problem is on your side; the reason most people don't feel close to God is because they are not trying to please Him. The Bible says that if you draw nigh to God that He will draw nigh to you. The truth is the reason that people don't feel close to God is because they have been living to please themselves, and that brings an emptiness, a void in your soul because there is a spot inside of us that only God can fill. Pleasing

Him will bring total satisfaction to you.

"I don't feel close to my husband or to my wife." Well, it is not on your mate's side; it is on the person that said it to start trying to please and watch your relationship with your mate blossom into something beautiful. It will draw you close to each other. The person that says I don't know you has just decreed that they have not taken time to spend time with the person that they said they did not know. That means a wife might have to go to that ball game or work on that car and that husband is going to have to go shopping and to that play that she wants to see. It is when we begin to do those things that the person feels free to share. It had nothing to do with the ball game at all; it had to do with you, **you were there**. We must realize that physical intimacy is the lowest form of intimacy, for you can be intimate with your spouse on that level and still not know what they really want. This is what is wrong with most men; we should know our mates past a soulish level, and that is where most women are. We must get into a spiritual intimacy; this is where true union and communion takes place, for the two shall become one, and this is not talking about sex. For God is a Spirit and we must know Him or worship Him in spirit and in truth. I don't have time to teach on marriage; this is about sonship. I pray that we can hear the voice of God. We must be willing to hang out with God on His terms, that we truly enjoy doing things His way, not because He is a mean God that will punish us, but because He is a Daddy that loves us, and to see Him pleased is what pleases you.

I pray that we know that the dog does not fetch the stick because he likes sticks. No, he fetches the stick because he thinks that it pleases you. That is why an owner must take the time to train the dog because it is a dog's nature to please, and he is at his best in doing that when he knows what you like. Otherwise he looks at you like you are stupid. If you feel distant, remember it is on your side because the Father loves you already. The Bible says that we love Him because He first loved us.

The last time the word Abba is used is in the book of Galatians. First let us read Galatians 3:23-29. It says, *But before faith came, we were kept under the law, shut up unto the faith which should afterwards be revealed. Wherefore the law was our* **schoolmaster** *to bring us unto Christ, that we might be justified by* **faith.** *But after that faith is come,* **we are no longer under a schoolmaster.** *For ye are* **all** *the* **children** *of God by faith in Christ Jesus. For as many of you as have been baptized into Christ have put on Christ.* **There is neither Jew nor Greek, there is neither bond nor free, there is neither male nor female: for ye are all one in Christ Jesus.** *And if ye be Christ's then are ye Abraham's seed, and heirs according to the promise.*

Lock in now. Galatians 4:1-7 says this, *Now I say* (if you understand chapter three concerning the law, Christ and the schoolmaster), *That the* **heir,** *as long as he is a* **CHILD,** *differeth nothing from a* **servant,** *though he be* **lord of all;** (even though it belongs to you, God said you can have none of it as long as you stay a child because a child in God's eyes is no different from a servant, and remember, servants do not have an inheritance.) *But is under* **tutors and governors** *until the time* **appointed** *of the* **Father.**

You see, it is not men that you have to please but the Father. He knows when you and I are ready. We know how to play the religious games, give our tithes, say amen. Husbands and wives will even hug each other in church, and before they can get into their car, they

99

are arguing with each other. You see, we might fool each other, but we are not fooling God. Then we begin to say to Him, "I'm ready," but we must remember that the appointment is on His side, and He says, "No, I can't adopt you yet; you are not ready."

All of the visions and dreams are true, all of the prophecies are true, but the appointment and fulfillment of that is in the Father's hand. We speed up or delay the prophecies over our lives. Jesus said if you would have known the time of your visitation you would have made yourself ready, and the Father has visitation rights anytime He wants them because you are His child. *Even so we, when we were* **children,** *were in bondage under the elements of the world. But when the fulness of the time was come, God sent forth His son, made of a woman, made under the law, To redeem them that were under the law, that we might* **receive** *the* **adoption of sons.** *And because ye are sons, God hath sent forth* **the Spirit of His Son** *into your hearts, Crying,* **Abba, Father.**

(What is the son's cry **ABBA?** Sons are the ones that have intimacy; sons are the ones that long to please Daddy. When He is grieved, they are grieved. There is such a sensitivity in the spirit with God that you know when His heart hurts or when He was satisfied with what was going on. That's when we can say as sons, Abba, Father.)

Wherefore thou art no more a servant but a **son;** *and if a* **son,** *then an* **heir of God through Christ.**

I wonder how many of us are ready to be sons, how many of us really want to grow up, how many of us want to receive the adoption, how many of us are ready to receive our inheritance.

Let us pray. ***Our Father which art in Heaven, forgive us of our doubt and immaturity, and bring***

☆ Abba is found in the bible 3 times (New testament)
Abba - daddy

100

us into faith and maturity. Receive us into your bosom. We love you today, we cry Abba Father unto you and long to be in your presence and to do your will, and we thank you that you have not been holding anything back from us, that it is your pleasure to give us the kingdom. We lift you up and praise you today and thank you that we are in the right family, and for this we give you all of the glory, all of the honor and all of the praise in the wonderful majestic name of JESUS, amen.

* It's more important to be a worshipper than a Praiser - Because worshippers praise god for who he is & not just for what he's done.

Intimacy in the place of maturity
the maturity of a person & the relationship the person is in. Abba is a name in the new testament only used with sons. Intimacy is not found until we grow up.

_____

Bible faith, is to act on the scriptures one has knowledge of & knows.

Heart faith / head faith

heart faith - Believes & receives in the heart
(hearers & doers)

head faith - a person who mentally agrees
with god & his word but has the inability to
carry out when circumstances arrive (hearers only)

The roles of the tutors & governors

CHAPTER FIFTEEN

What About The Five-fold Ministry

IN THE BOOK OF GALATIANS 4:1-2, it reads, *Now I say, that the **heir**, as long as he is a **child**, **differeth nothing from a servant**, **though he be lord of all**; But is **under tutors and governors** until the time **appointed of the father**.*

What I want us to see is that the children are placed under someone, tutors and governors. The word tutor in this scripture means a servant, commissioner, domestic manager, guardian and steward. The word governor in this scripture means a house distributor, overseer, one in the capacity of treasurer, not just money but people. People are part of the true treasures of God, a preacher, chamberlain and steward. I like the fact that in both definitions they are both called stewards as part of their definitions. This is important because ministry gifts need to understand that we only have stewardship and not ownership. Everything and everyone that God places into our care belongs to HIM. But on the other hand, we can see that these tutors and governors are what we call the ministry listed in Ephesians chapter four. In Ephesians four we have the ministry gifts who they have been sent to and what they are supposed to do. Ephesians 4:1-3,7-8,11-16 reads, *I Therefore, the prisoner of the Lord, beseech you that ye walk worthy of the vocation wherewith ye are called, With all **lowliness** and **meekness**, with **longsuffering**,* *forbearing one another in love; Endeavouring to keep the unity of the Spirit in the bond of peace. But unto every one of us is given grace according to the measure of the gift of Christ Wherefore He saith, When He ascended up on high, He led captivity captive, and gave gifts unto men. And He gave some, apostles; and some, prophets; and some, evangelists; and some, pastors and teachers; For the perfecting of the saints, for the work of the ministry, for the edifying of the body of Christ: Till we all come in the unity of the faith, and of the knowledge of the Son of God, unto a perfect man, unto the measure of the stature of the fulness of Christ: That we henceforth be no more children, tossed to and fro, and carried about with every wind of doctrine, by the sleight of men, and cunning craftiness, whereby they lie in wait to deceive; But speaking the truth in love, may grow up into Him in all things, which is the head, even Christ: From whom the whole body fitly joined together and compacted by that which every joint supplieth, according to the effectual working in the measure of every part, maketh increase of the body unto the edifying of itself in love.*

God gave the five-fold ministry, or grace ministry, or hand ministry in verse 11, to people in verse eight. The ministry's responsibility is to cause the people to grow up. Verses 12 through 16 that we could have unity. Verses three and 13, now this is just a quick overview. We are going to go into much more detail, but we should understand by now why God wants us to grow up. We must also understand that we need the ministry in order to grow up; we must recognize that the ministry is the hands of God given to mold the clay of God that the clay can touch the heart of God and move with the Head of God by the Holy Ghost. Next to God, the name of

Jesus, the Word of God, the blood of the Lamb, the Holy Spirit and Christ Anointing, the ministry plays the biggest part in the development and maturity of the saints of God. The ministry is the only physical part of God's spiritual working that you can actually see. This is important because spirituality is always carried out in practicality.

For example, a person will say that I am under God's authority. Well, not if you are not under the delegated authority that you can see. The Bible says in first John 4:20, *If a man say, I love God, and hateth his brother, he is a liar: for he that loveth not his brother whom he hath seen, how can he love God whom he hath not seen?*

All I am saying is spirituality has a very practical side or outworking that is done by faith. Now I will treat this subject with great care and balance, but we have an enemy called the devil, and he knows that if he can keep God's people out of church, then he can keep them from their inheritance. What he has done is convince so many believers that they don't need the church, specifically the local church, and people base that on being hurt in their local church. But I have come to find out that most of what we call being hurt really means that a person is saying that I did not get my way; now I am not making light of anything I just want us to understand that we cannot grow up without the ministry. God has commissioned the ministry to help us to grow up because growing up is the only way that we receive our inheritance, so I will allow the scriptures to speak for themselves. And let us remember that authority and submission is not the end of a thing; it is the beginning of a thing; it is God's desire that out of authority and submission will come harmony and unity, so everything that I say here I say from the standpoint of maturity and unity from reconciliation, and not condemnation. We must remember that Christ is the Head of the church, and while I am here Christ is also the Head of the home. Understanding this will help us. Every ministry gift only has authority because they are under authority, and being under authority is why ministry has authority. It is not of themselves; it comes from God as we will see later, Matthew 8:5-10 reads, *And when Jesus was entered into Capernaum, there came unto him a centurion, beseeching him, And saying, Lord, my servant lieth at home sick of the palsy, grievously tormented. And Jesus saith unto him, I will come and heal him. The centurion answered and said, Lord, I am not worthy that thou shouldest come **under** my roof: but **speak the word only**, and my servant shall be healed. For I am a man **under authority**, having soldiers **under** me: and I say to this man, Go, and he goeth; and to another, Come, and he cometh; and to my servant, Do this, and he doeth it. When Jesus heard it, He marvelled, and said to them that followed, Verily I say unto you, I have not found so great **faith**, no, not in Israel.*

I pray that we can see that the only reason that the man had authority is because he was under authority, Jesus equated him understanding the laws of authority to faith, a faith that all you have to do is speak and things happen. Well, that is what the ministry does, they speak. First Corinthians 12:18,28 says, *But now hath God set the members every one of them in the body, as it hath **pleased** him. And God hath set some in the church, first apostles, secondarily prophets, thirdly teachers, after that miracles, then gifts of healings, helps, governments, diversities of tongues.*

God is the one that sets people in the church, and Christ is the head of the church. Malachi 3:18, 4:6, and First Corinthians 4:15 reads, *And they shall be mine, saith the Lord of hosts, in that day when I make up my jewels; and I will spare them. as a man spareth his own son that serveth him. And he shall turn the heart of the fathers to the children, and the heart of the children to their fathers, lest I come and smite the earth with a curse. For though ye have ten thousand instructers in Christ, yet have ye not many fathers: for in Christ Jesus I have begotten you through the gospel.*

The people of God are the jewels of God, and He is not just letting anyone speak into your heart. The ministry is always speaking from the heart of a father or one who wants the best for you; the ministry is never trying to argue or make a point. No, we speak out of the love of the Father. That word instructor there means a young playful one or one that takes you to the school but not a teacher in the school. Authority and submission is learned at the hands of God's seasoned ministers, not by an instructor or novice trying to show you how many scriptures they can quote, but by people under the Holy Spirit that truly care about your life, amen.

Though a minister may be in a position of leadership or authority, they are always on the grounds of unity, and endeavoring to keep that unity. Not understanding these spiritual laws and principles of connection will always leave one, two steps away from all that God has for you. For God's way is the way of assembly, leading and following, authority and submission, and if the devil can keep you away from these truths, he can keep you away from your inheritance. We don't like to talk about this because we didn't know the answer, but now we do. The answer is not in authority; it is in unity, but the door into the room of unity is authority. It is God's desire that the line between authority and submission be erased and vanishes that there is not two but a merging into one. Unity is where one partakes in the blessing of another, we must receive Jesus as Lord before we receive God as Father. Unity is where God commands the blessing.

Look at these scriptures with me, Luke 6:46, John 17:20-23, John 13:34-35, Ephesians 4:3, Hebrews 10:23-25, Psalm 133:1-3. Jesus said, *And why call ye me, Lord, Lord, and do not the things which I say? Neither pray I for these alone, but for them also which shall believe on me through their word; That they all may be one; as thou, Father, art in me, and I in thee, that they also may be one in us: that the world may believe that thou hast sent me. And the glory which thou gavest me I have given them; that they may be one, even as we are one: I in them, and thou in me, that they may be made perfect in one; and that the world may know that thou hast sent me, and hast loved them, as thou hast loved me. A new commandment I give unto you, That ye love one another; as I have loved you, that ye also love one another. By this shall all men know that ye are my disciples* (learned ones), *if ye have love one to another. Endeavouring to keep the unity of the Spirit in the bond of peace.* (Not make unity but keep unity in the bond of peace). *Let us hold fast the profession of our faith without wavering; (for He is faithful that promised;) And let us consider one another to provoke unto love and to good works: Not forsaking the assembling of ourselves together, as the manner of some is; but exhorting one another: and so much the more, as ye see the day approaching. Behold, how good and how pleasant it is for* **brethren to dwell together in unity!** *It is like the precious ointment upon the head, that ran down upon the beard, even Aaron's beard: that went down to the skirts of his garments; As the dew of Hermon, and as the dew that descended upon the mountains of Zion:* **for there the**

Unity is where God commands the blessing. As ministers it is our responsibility to teach the rule and not the exception to the rule, because wit in the structure of the rule is where the blessing is. But so many Christians try to live in the exception and end up in deception and find themselves on a false foundation. Ministry is not out for control; that's the devil and the flesh. No, we establish order. The Bible talks about disorder, the due order, and doing things decently and in order. First Corinthians 14:40 says, *Let **all** things be done decently and in order.*

One of the ways we begin to grow up and mature is we begin again to walk in the rule and not the exception. Talent can be developed alone but character, Godly character, specifically the character of Christ, can only be developed in everyday life, and that primarily in the local church. This is why one can be a great athlete but in life be a failure because they have no character. Well, this also happens with God's people. They refuse to allow God to develop them in the local church, but they are failing in life. People of God, the base of life is balance, and balance is found in the WORD OF GOD, and that is what the ministers of God have been called to preach. We are talking about going from infancy to maturity, from failure to a finisher, from glory to glory, from conception to perfection, from faith to faith. Where we start is not where we are supposed to finish. Many are called but few are chosen. You don't know how many people tell me that they are called. "I'm called, I'm called, I'm called." Good, so is everyone else. The question is, have you been chosen? Most people flunk out of the school of the Holy Ghost where He is the Dean, Chancellor and the Teacher, but He uses men in the local church. It is here that we go from babies to sons;

it is here that the choosing takes place. If we don't pass the test in the local church with the governors and tutors, God is unable to receive you unto Himself, to impart to you your full inheritance. Our drop-out percentage has been too high; it is time for us to re-enroll into school, a good local church, and those that are in school, our grades have been too low.

Look at Proverbs 20:3-7 with me. *It is an honour for a man to cease from strife: but every fool will be meddling. The sluggard will not plow by reason of the cold; therefore shall he beg in harvest, and have nothing. Counsel in the heart of man is like deep water; but a man of understanding will draw it out. Most men will proclaim every one his own goodness: but a faithful man who can find? The just man walketh in his integrity: his children are blessed after him.*

Well, what is the Lord saying to us in these verses? One, too many people argue the word instead of receiving it, or they hear it but don't do it and end up with nothing. People have visions in them, but they don't know how to get it out of them, and this is why we have the ministry. They have been ordained of God to help us get out what is deep in us. Too many people are bragging about how great they are and how perfect they are and how right and never wrong they are, but never seek a confirmation on it. The measure of that person is how faithful are they to someone else's work, ministry, or business, because faithfulness is the mark of greatness and maturity. Faithfulness will cause others to say good things about you so you won't have to do it yourself. And a man of character walks upright, and that is seen not just in him but in his family. A man of integrity does not just talk right, he walks right.

Look with me at the book of Ruth 1:1-5,20-21, *Now it came to pass in the days when the judges ruled, that there was a famine in the land. And a certain man of Beth-le-hem-ju-dah* (which means the place of bread and praise or where you receive the Word and where you worship which in the local church) *went to sojourn in the country of Moab* (which means washpot), *he, and his wife, and his two sons. And the name of the man was Elimelech* (which means that God is King), *and the name of his wife Naomi* (which means God's delight), *and the name of his two sons Mahlon and Chilion* (which means sickly and weakly), *Ephrathites of Bethlehem-judah. And they came into the country of Moab, and continued there. And Elimelech Naomi's husband died; and she was left, and her two sons. And they took them wives of the women of Moab; the name of the one was Orpah, and the name of the other Ruth: and they dwelled there about ten years. And Mahlon and Chilion died also both of them; and the woman was left of her two sons and her husband. And she said unto them, Call me not Naomi, call me Mara: for the Almighty hath dealt very bitterly with me. I went out full, and the Lord hath brought me home again empty: why then call ye me Naomi, seeing the Lord hath testified against me, and the Almighty hath afflicted me?*

This is going on all around the body of Christ that people are in the right place, but things don't seem to be going their way, so first they stop doing what they should and then they leave, and when you get outside the will of God for your life things start messing up, and that's what happened. All the flaws came forth, and they died out there. As long as you are where you are supposed to be and doing what you are supposed to do, your flaws never show, praise God. People are losing their homes, their jobs, their families and marriages, all because things didn't look well where they where. Some people leave churches because they think they're going to get a better job. But most people leave because things are not going their way and they are going to prove to those around them that they are right, but very few people leave because God said so. Remember, they left because there was a famine in the land, but not a famine in their land. They were in the church, the church that God wanted them in, and they were blessed and did not know it because the Bible says that when they left they were full, but when she came back she was empty and bitter and blamed God. This is what people do; they get outside the will of God whether they leave or stay, and things start messing up and they blame God, their shepherd and everyone else when it is them that's out of the will of God, so where you go to church is very important. There is a bethlehem-judah for you, and that place is where your blessing is. She went home, and if you read the rest of the book, she received her inheritance. How about you, you too are GOD'S DE-LIGHT. I pray that we understand that we can't make it alone.

Let us look at some more scriptures, II Timothy 1:9-11, II Timothy 3:16-17, II Timothy 4:1-4, Acts 20-27-32, and I Peter 5:1-4. *Who hath saved us, and called us with an holy calling, not according to our **works,** but according to his own **purpose** and grace, which was given us in Christ Jesus before the world began. But is now made manifest by the appearing of our Savior Jesus Christ, who hath abolished death, and hath brought life and immortality to light through the gospel; Whereunto I am appointed a preacher, and an apostle, and a teacher of the Gentiles.*

(The minister is one who receives a holy calling and a divine appointment from God. This is nothing that you aspire to like being a doctor. No, God must call you and appoint you to the ministry.)

All scripture is given by inspiration of God, and is profitable for doctrine, for reproof, for correction, for instruction in righteousness: that the man of God may be perfect, thoroughly furnished unto all good works. I Charge thee therefore before God, and the Lord Jesus Christ, who shall judge the quick and the dead at his appearing and his kingdom; Preach the word; be instant in season, out of season; reprove, rebuke, exhort with all longsuffering and doctrine. For the time will come when they will not endure sound doctrine; but after their own lusts shall they heap to themselves teachers, having itching ears; And they shall turn away their ears from the truth, and shall be turned unto fables. For I have not shunned to declare unto you all the counsel of God. Take heed therefore unto yourselves, and to all the flock, over the which the Holy Ghost hath made you overseers, to feed the church of God, which he hath purchased with his own blood. For I know this, that after my departing shall grievous wolves enter in among you, not sparing the flock, Also of your own selves shall men arise, speaking perverse things, to draw away disciples after them. Therefore watch, and remember, that by the space of three years I ceased not to warn everyone night and day with tears. And now, brethren, I commend you to God, and to the word of his grace, which is able to build you up, and to give you an inheritance among all them which are sanctified. The elders which are among you I exhort, who am also an elder, and a witness of the sufferings of Christ, and also a partaker of the glory that shall be revealed: Feed the flock of God which is among you, taking the oversight thereof, not by constraint, but willingly: not for filthy lucre, but of a ready mind; Neither as being lords over God's heritage, but being ensamples to the flock. And when the chief Shepherd shall appear, ye shall receive a crown of glory that fadeth not away.

What the ministry of God-appointed ministers endeavors to do is preach the word when people want to hear and when they don't, because the word is the balance and the rule. This is where safety and success is. The scriptures are the ground of authority that the minister has to walk on, so if you go to a church that opens up the Bible, that is a good thing. We must also see that the ministry is given in the local church for spiritual guidance and spiritual covering, protection and oversight. The ministry is set in place by God, not to lord over you, but to be an example unto you, not in just what we say, but in what we do. SEE Acts 1:1.

A seasoned minister is one who cares and has dedicated their life to God and the spiritual growth of others. I would dare say that no one on this earth with the exception of your parents cares about you more than God-ordained ministers. I say these things because there is integrity and honor in the ministry, so don't let satan stop you from being a part of the body of Christ and a good local church, which is where the blessing of God is. Every great man or women of God was submitted to someone, Elijah and Elisha, Moses and Joshua, Paul and Timothy, Jesus and the twelve. Let us remember that Elisha had a servant or young follower and his name was Gehazi, but he did wrong (he always did his own thing) and never received the anointing, and Elisha's anointing stayed with him even in death. All true ministers of God have been tried and tested and have sat up under someone else's authority and been proved, for God would not allow just anyone to speak to you. Some company might put a rookie in leadership, but God never does. And my dear brothers and sisters, the anointing still flows from the head down. We must be faithful in that which is another man's, or

God will not give us that which is our own, and this is part of the purpose of the local church. The principles that the ministry would try to get you to walk in are principles they are walking in themselves, for God does not allow you to lead if you are unwilling to follow. I am not against conferences or special meetings. I have been to a few myself, but satan has made the body of Christ think that they can go to a conference and be sustained, and you can't. The conference only enhances and confirms the work that is going on in the local church that God has you, or should I say, wants you to be a part of. But the special meetings are not ordained of God to replace the local church. You see, in the special meeting you can go and not know anyone. You don't have to be accountable to anyone, but neither is anyone accountable for you. You can't develop spiritually like that; the local church is like an old-fashioned doctor. We still make house calls and will tell you the truth.

Jesus is building His church, but He does that according to new testament order which is through a local church where people can come and grow. This is why many times after a conference you find God's people go through spiritual withdrawal, because they don't have a local church to go to, to be trained and continue with what they heard in a conference or special meeting to be taught how to carry that out in a practical way in everyday life. Television and special meetings are ordained, but not ordained to take the place of that local church where correction and instruction takes place.

Look at these scriptures with me, Romans 10:13-17, James 1:19-24, Hebrews 13:7,17,24, Romans 13:1-2, Luke 10:16, John 13:20, II Timothy 2:1-5 I Corinthians 4:1-2, and Luke 16:12. *For whosoever shall call upon the name of the LORD shall be saved. How then shall they call on him in whom they have not believed?*

And how shall they believe in him of whom they have not heard? And how shall they **hear** *without a* **preacher?** *And how shall they* **preach, except they be sent?** *as it is written, How beautiful are the feet of them that* **preach** *the gospel of peace, and bring glad tidings of good things! But they have not all* **obeyed** *the gospel. For Isaiah saith, Lord, who hath believed our report? So then* **faith cometh by hearing,** *and* **hearing by the word of God.** *Wherefore, my beloved brethren, let every man be swift to* **hear,** *slow to speak, slow to wrath: For the wrath of man worketh not the righteousness of God. Wherefore lay apart all filthiness and superfluity of naughtiness, and receive with meekness the engrafted* **word,** *which is able to save your* **souls.** *But be ye* **doers** *of the* **word,** *and* **not hearers only,** *deceiving your own selves. For if any be a* **hearer** *of the word, and not a* **doer,** *he is like unto a man beholding his natural face in a glass: For he beholdeth himself, and goeth his way, and straightway forgetteth what manner of man he was. Remember them which have the* **rule** *over you, who have spoken unto you the word of God: whose faith* **follow,** *considering the end of their conversation (life).* **Obey** *them that have the* **rule** *over you, and* **submit** *yourselves:* **for they watch for your souls,** *as they that* **must give account,** *that they may do it with joy, and not with grief: for that is unprofitable for you. Salute all them that have the* **rule** *over you, and all the saints. They of Italy salute you. Let every soul be* **subject** *unto the higher powers. For there is no power but of God: the powers that be are* **ordained of God.** *Whosoever therefore resisteth the power, resisteth the ordinance of God: and they that resist shall receive to themselves damnation. He that* **heareth you heareth me;** *and he that despiseth you despiseth me; and he that despiseth me despiseth him that sent me.*

Verily, verily, I say unto you, **He that receiveth whomsoever I send receiveth me;** *and he that receiveth me receiveth him that sent me. Thou therefore, my son, be strong in the grace that is in Christ Jesus. And the things that thou hast* **heard** *of me among many witnesses, the same commit thou to* **faithful** *men, who shall be able to teach others also. thou therefore endure hardness, as a good soldier of Jesus Christ. No man that warreth entangleth himself with the affairs of this life; that he may please him who hath* **chosen** *him to be a soldier. And if a man also strive for masteries, yet is he not crowned, except he strive lawfully* (plays according to the rules). *Let a man so account of us, as of the ministers of Christ, and* **stewards of the mysteries of God.** *Moreover it is required in* **stewards,** *that a man be found* **faithful.** *And if ye have not been* **faithful** *in that which is* **another man's** *who shall give you that which is* **your own?**

So God is saying unto us that we must listen and do what the ministry is teaching us to do, and on top of that be faithful to, because they are giving us the rules and watching out for our souls and sharing the truth with us. The ministry assists God in bringing the people their faith because our faith comes to us by hearing those who have been chosen, ordained, and sent by God. Let us remember that there is no ministry without Christ, and there is no message without a man to speak it. It is called humility. So many people want God's head (his mind) and even desire his heart and dare to pray for his honor, but we fail to recognize that God does this by his hands which is the ministry.

I Peter 5:5-7 says, *Likewise, ye younger, submit yourselves unto the elder. Yea, all of you be subject one to another, and be clothed with humility: for GOD resisteth the proud, and giveth grace to the humble. Humble your-*

selves (God is not going to make you and neither is the ministry; you must do it yourself) *therefore under the mighty hand of God, that he may exalt you in due time: Casting all your care upon him; for he careth for you.* God will always make sure that the word coming forth from the pulpit touches you and is applicable to your life because he cares for you, but it is up to you to receive it. God gave us the ministry so we could qualify in stewardship to those that we see in order to receive the benefits of sonship from Him that we can only see by faith. Remember that the ministry cannot make anyone do anything, the ministry can only lead those that will follow. The Apostle Paul said, "Follow me as I follow Christ." I write these things not that ministry can lord over you but because I care and want you blessed, and the blessing is in the process. That if we humble ourselves God will exalt us, and the Bible says that promotion comes from the Lord. See Psalms 75:6-7.

Psalms 22:22, Jeremiah 30:21, Numbers 16:5, Acts 13:1-2 and Hebrews 2:12} reads, *I will declare thy name unto my brethren: in the midst of the **congregation** will I praise thee. And their nobles shall be of **themselves** and their governor shall proceed from the **midst** of them; and I will cause him to draw near, and he shall approach unto me: for who is this that engaged his heart* (who is this that cares) *to approach unto me? saith the LORD. And he spake unto Korah and unto all his company, saying, Even tomorrow the LORD will shew who are his, and who is holy; and will cause him to come near unto him: even him whom he hath chosen will he cause to come near unto him. Now there were in the church that was at Antioch certain prophets and teachers; as Barnabas, and Simeon that was called Niger, and Lucius of Cyrene, and Manaen, which had been brought up with Herod the tetrarch, and Saul* (this is the Apostle Paul). *As they ministered to the Lord, and fasted, the Holy Ghost said,* **Separate** *me Barnabas and Saul for the* **work** *whereunto I have called them. Saying, I will declare thy name unto my brethren, in the midst of the* **church** *will I sing praise unto thee.*

True ministry gifts also receive their training in the local church where there spiritual gifting can be judged, where anointing from God, wisdom and integrity are important, not academic education, but biblical Holy Spirit revelation God breathed teaching. See Acts 4:13. Not just knowledge that puffs up, but an unction to function where a minister learns to hear and do, and you cannot teach what you have not, would not or are not doing. See Acts 1:1. True ministers don't have a superiority complex, but one of humility and servanthood. To this person though they are leading, they realize they themselves are being led and so lead by example and not just in word only but in action. We understand that all of God's people are precious, important and priceless and that we are all equal but have different priorities and functions in the kingdom of God. The ministry sees the people's social, economical and political surroundings, but our primary responsibility is one's spiritual condition before God, having confidence that if that is right all the other things will fall into place. For when people come to God, they come with broken hearts, broken homes, failed marriages, ego problems, drug problems, criminal problems, money problems and such where some of us but God through the ministry and the anointing of the Holy Spirit has made us productive in our homes, our churches and our communities. This you cannot put a price on. And some would dare to say that you can't trust the ministry or say that the ministry does not care, when it was God that says, "Come as you are, I love you." See Luke 4:18-19, Acts

10:38, I Corinthians 6:11, I Thessalonians 5:23, III John :2.

I pray that we do not forget that this is still a vocation whose focus always has been on people about ministry (serving) and not money, that is about helping and not hurting, hope and not hopelessness. The ministry is about God sharing His heart by using His anointed hands (the ministry). Let us remember that the ministry is not greater but graced to serve. Our primary responsibility is not to tell you what you can't do, but tell you what you can do and with the anointing of God charge you to do what you could not and did not have the strength to do before. Philippians 4:13 says, *I* (we) *can do all things through Christ which strengtheneth me.*

The ministry is the only living organism that has been ordained and anointed by God to do real spiritual work, that is only found in the Body of Christ, practically carried out in the local church. I would encourage you, like Naomi, you don't have to be empty; you can be full; come home.

CHAPTER SIXTEEN

The Cocoon Factor

IN EARLIER CHAPTERS we dealt with the word become, and we used the caterpillar, that he goes from a caterpillar to a butterfly, and we said that it was the caterpillar's destiny to become or emerge as a butterfly. That where he started in life is not where he was supposed to finish. But there is something that we need to talk about that I believe is very important, and that is the cocoon factor.

First Corinthians chapter 2:9-16 says, *But as it is written, Eye hath not seen, nor ear heard, neither have entered into the heart of man, the things which GOD hath prepared for them that love Him. But God hath revealed them unto us by His Spirit: for the Spirit searcheth all things, yea, the deep things of God. For what man knoweth the things of a man, save the spirit of man which is in him: even so the things of God knoweth no man, but the Spirit of God. Now we have received, not the spirit of the world, but the spirit which is of God; that we might know the things that are freely given to us of God. Which things also we speak, not in the words which man's wisdom teacheth, but which the Holy Ghost teacheth; comparing spiritual things with spiritual. But the natural man receiveth not the things of the Spirit of God: for they are foolishness unto him: neither can he know them, because they are spiritually discerned. But he that is spiritual judgeth all things, yet he himself is judged of no man. For who hath known the mind of the Lord, that he may instruct him? But we have the mind of Christ.*

These things that we share we share by the Holy Ghost out of the mind of Christ, understanding fully that we have the life of God in us by the operation of the Holy Spirit. We set forth these truths under the unction of the anointing of God. Now what is the cocoon factor? It is this: the caterpillar knows that in order to fly there is a death principle involved; he understands that he cannot fly unless he experiences the death principle. This is the cocoon factor. This could be defined in so many ways; for some it is simply to move out of your comfort zone and doing this would bring change to you. For others they have to have what we call a near death experience before they see life through different eyes and begin to live from a different perspective. Most businesses and ministries never start or get off the ground until they experience this principle. These examples could be defined as the cocoon factor, but I believe that, biblically speaking, there is a lot more to it than just this, and that is what we want to talk about. The caterpillar understands this thing. It involves death; it is a real thing and a real decision. He must make his own grave; he forms it himself and knows that if he ever wants to become a butterfly he has to participate in the cocoon factor. It is not something that anyone makes him do; he does it on his own if he wants to fly. What are we dealing with? We are dealing with the death, burial and resurrection of a thing. We cannot try to be like Christ; Christ himself must be formed in us (as we choose to die to self), blessing us and equipping us to do what we in our own strength could not do before.

Romans 5:6 says, *For when we were yet without strength, in due time Christ died for the ungodly.*

So when we begin to say that we need to be more like Christ or act more like Jesus, we are not talking about imitating Him; we are talking about His very life coming forth through you and me. It is Christ himself. Christianity is not a religion, Christianity is a life, and that life is in the Person of God's son, the Lord Jesus himself, He Is Alive. And so we must deal with the cocoon factor because it is within the cocoon factor, or we will struggle with the process of the butterfly. The caterpillar, as long as he is a caterpillar, no matter how hard he tries to fly, he can't. He may look at the rest of his family and see them flying, and he may even crawl up a tree and jump from the tree and try to fly, but he is going to land back on the ground again. It does not matter how high he climbs up the tree; gravity is going to take effect on him because he is not equipped with his wings. He does not have the ability to fly no matter how hard he thinks it, no matter how hard he tries, no matter how much he wishes it, he cannot fly unless he goes into the cocoon. There is no way around this, so for you and I to become, we have to willingly choose just like the caterpillar to inch along. Until he gets to his grave, he is inching toward his grave. Why? Because he knows that if he can just get there and settle the issue once and for all that I in myself can do nothing. I cannot fly; no matter how hard I try, I can't, so what do I do? The cocoon factor. I am going to make my grave day after day and get in there and wait for my transformation. Then I am going to come out of the grave, and it is going to be me, but it is not going to be me. I know that it is me, but there is something different about me. I used to walk on the ground, but now I know intuitively and spiritually it's not me. If I step outside of this cocoon I know I can fly. It's me, but it's a different me. I can go higher now; I can go further now; I can get there quicker now. Why? Because I have experienced the cocoon factor. Something happens there.

Galatians 4:19 says, *My little children, of whom I travail in birth again until Christ be formed in you.*

Christ must be formed in us. This word formed is only used four times in the new testament. This word in the Greek is Morphoo, which means to change and form. Now when Christ is in you and me He morphoos us. In Romans 12:2 the word transformed is used, and that is the Greek word metamorphoo. When you and I choose the cocoon, inwardly Christ is forming and outwardly you are transforming into ... The more Christ is formed in you, the more you and people see the transformation; truly there is a metamorphosis happening. You see, without the life of Christ in you, and you yielding to that life, you will never become.

This is why religion in and of itself has never changed anyone; only life has the power to transform a person, and Jesus said that I came that you might have life and life more abundantly. He came to give you more than you ever had before. But His life only comes forth through the cocoon factor as long as it is just me. The only me that I can be is a caterpillar; that's it, but when Christ gets into it, everything changes. In the eyes of God, objectively speaking, everything is already done. God declares the end from the beginning He does not start until He is finished, but subjectively speaking it is not finished. There is something happening subjectively by the Holy Ghost inside of you and me, constantly, consistently and continually, so God always speaks to us according to who we are and not according to what we are going to be, because to Him **WE ARE!!**

God always speaks to us according to a finished work, not that it's going to happen, but that it has already happened. Then we see what He sees and we say, "God, I am not there. God, that's not real; I must be dreaming, and if you tell someone what you saw they will tell you that you must have been dreaming. Because they only see you from where you are right now, but they cannot see the blueprint of how to get you to your dream in God.

You see, we must come into agreement with God and not try and fulfill the dream alone. Don't try to use your own strength and might or you will falter and fail in the fight, instead of fly and soar like an eagle in the sky. God is saying objectively, it is done, but we say objectively, it is not done. So what did God do? He sent forth His SON into our lives, and by the power of the Holy Spirit subjectively we are being formed into the son of God on a daily basis. His life is coming forth in us, and it happens a certain way. How does it happen? Through the cocoon factor, so by faith we call those things that be not as though they were and boldly decree I AM what God said I AM!!!

This is something that we choose to do daily. What is that? DIE to self and our own way and go God's way. This is not something that your mentor can make you do, your boss, husband or wife can make you do; you must choose on your own to go to the cocoon. If you don't make it to the cocoon, you will never fly, which is your destiny. Please don't put it off; start heading toward the cocoon right now, because the joy, beauty and total fulfillment of your life is on the other side of the cocoon. There are Christians that are on this earth right now, they are children, God loves them, God has accepted them into the beloved, but they never grow up and become sons. Some people stay caterpillars their entire Christian life because they never choose to go. Every day we must make a cautious decision that I am not going my way; I am going God's way. As soon as I make that decision, the more His life comes forth in me the life that holds eternity.

Galatians 2:20-21 says, *I am crucified with Christ: nevertheless I live; yet not I, but Christ liveth in me: and the life which I now live in the flesh I live by the faith of the Son of God, who loved me, and gave himself for me. I do not frustrate the grace of God: for if righteousness come by the law, then Christ is dead in vain.*

Now this goes back to the caterpillar. The caterpillar looks at his life after he comes out of the cocoon, and he says I know this is me but it's not me; this is a different me. I am alive right now in Christ, but outwardly I look like the same guy I was before I died in Christ or before I accepted Jesus Christ as my Lord and Savior. I know for myself that I am changed. I am different; I am me, but I am a different me because of Christ. Read Galatians 2:20-21 again so all of the goodness, grace and love that is in me, is not me but Christ in me, so all of the glory for my life goes to God. So there is no bragging on myself because it is not me, even though it is me, but it is not me but Christ inside of me.

A person who begins to talk like this is a person who has experienced the cocoon factor. It is God's desire that we finish what we start in life and not be failures. See Philippians 1:6 and Hebrews 12:1-2. Yet so many people try to run this race of life without God's help, and if we would be truthful most people are failing in more than one area of our life, when God wants you blessed in every part of your life. How does this happen? We must start toward the cocoon and yield our lives to God. Look at what the bible says you have to do in order to bring forth much fruit or be prosperous or have a big harvest.

John 12:23-24 says, *And Jesus answered them, saying, The hour is come, that the Son of man should be glorified. Verily, verily, I say unto you, Except a corn of wheat fall into the ground and* **die,** *it abideth* **alone** (you bring forth nothing): *but if it* **die,** *it bringeth forth* **much fruit.**

So the bible is clear; in order to bring forth fruit we must die. God has given us the power to become more than you ever dreamed possible. People will ask the question, what came first, the chicken or the egg? This is an easy question when you see things from God's prospective. The chicken came first; it could not have been the egg. Why? Because the Bible says in Genesis 1:11-12,21-22,24-25, *And God said, Let the earth bring forth* **grass,** *the herb* **yielding seed,** *and the* **fruit tree yielding fruit after his kind, whose seed is in itself,** *upon the earth: and it was so. And the earth brought forth* **grass, and herb yielding seed after his kind, and the tree yielding fruit, whose seed was IN itself, after his kind:** *and God saw that it was good. And God* **created** *great whales, and every living creature that moveth, which the waters brought forth abundantly,* **after their kind,** *and every* **winged fowl after his kind:** *and God saw that it was good. And God blessed them, saying,* **Be** *fruitful, and multiply, and fill the waters in the seas, and let fowl multiply in the earth. And God said, Let the earth bring forth the living creature* **after his kind, cattle, and creeping thing, and beast of the earth after his kind:** *and it was so. And God* **made the beast of the earth after his kind, and cattle after their kind,** *and every thing that creepeth upon the earth after his kind: and God saw that it was good.*

This is why we know that the chicken came first

and not the egg, because God said that He has given everything that He made power to produce seed after its own kind. Now if we understand this principle, if God would have made the egg first, then the only thing that it could ever become is an egg. This is the reason that we know that Adam had to be a full-grown man when God made and created him is because if he was just a little boy, the best that we could have ever become is a little boy, but Adam was a man and God equipped him to produce seed after his own kind.

I don't mean to play hardball, but this throws Darwin's theory, not fact, of evolution out the window and allows God's truth to stand. And that truth is if you want apples you must plant apple seeds that came from an apple tree, and if you want a human being you must have human seed (sperm) and if we are supposed to be like anyone, we are supposed to act like and be like God. God speaks to us according to who we are and not where we are, so we can stop thinking that we come from fish, birds, snakes or monkeys. These thoughts are beneath us and a slap in the face to God.

Look at Genesis 1:26-28: *And God said, Let us make man in our image, after our likeness: and let them have dominion over the fish of the sea, and over the fowl of the air, and over the cattle, and over all the earth, and over every creeping thing that creepeth upon the earth. So God **created man in his own image,** in the image of God created he him; male and female **created** he them. And God blessed them, and God said unto them, Be fruitful, and multiply, and replenish the earth, and subdue it: and have dominion over the fish of the sea, and over the fowl of the air, and over every living thing that moveth upon the earth.*

God has given us power to become sons of God!!! First Peter 1:23-25 says, *Being born again, not of cor-*

*ruptible **seed,** but of incorruptible, by the **word of God,** which liveth and abideth for ever. For all flesh is as grass, and all the glory of man as the flower of grass. The grass withereth, and the flower thereof falleth away: But **the word of the LORD endureth for ever. And this is the word which by the gospel is preached unto you.***

God knows that through the spoken word, which the Bible calls the incorruptible seed (sperm) that gets in our heart and changes our lives from glory to glory. Well, the word comes from God, and the word is the seed, so the only thing that you and I can become is what He is and God has given you and I the power to become if we believe. **YOU ARE SO MUCH MORE THAN YOU THINK YOU ARE.**

First John 4:17 says, *Herein is our love made perfect, that we may have boldness in the day of judgment:* ***BECAUSE AS HE IS SO ARE WE IN THIS WORLD!***

God has given us the power to become by the seed that He places in us. What is the seed that he has placed in us: the seed of His SON through the WORD OF GOD. God gave us His word that we can become what He IS. Let us remember that it is the butterfly that lays its eggs or its larvae; it is not the caterpillar, it is the butterfly, so the only reason that the caterpillar can **become** a butterfly is because it came from a butterfly. He only starts as a caterpillar, but he does not finish there. So the butterfly lays its eggs and then it becomes larvae and then a caterpillar, and now he sees the rest of his family flying, and he says I want to fly, too. And the family says to him, "You know what you have to do, don't you? And there he goes inching along toward the cocoon factor. If you want to be transformed into a butterfly, you have to go to the cocoon first, and this is seen all through the Word of God that we choose God's way daily. And as we choose God's way, what we are doing is dying to our **own way,** dying to self. The Bible says that our ways are not His ways. See Isaiah 55:7-9. God gave us eyes and said don't look, gave us hands and said don't touch, gave us a mouth and said don't say a word. These things are hard to do when someone has been wrong to you. God says that the way up is by going down.

These principles make no sense to the carnal man, but we are not those that are carnal, we are **spiritual** in our constitution and make-up, amen. The more you die to self by choosing God's way, the more you are becoming what He is, and when people see you they see Christ. Christianity is not something that we practice on Sunday. No, it is something that we have experienced and lived on Monday, and this is what people must see. They must see us live this life and not just have a religious form of it. Maturity is not conceivable without Christ; this is all about Him.

Colossians 1:25-27 says, *Whereof I am made a minister, according to the dispensation of God which is given to me for you, to fulfil the word of God; Even the **mystery** which hath been hid from ages and from generations, but now is made manifest to his saints: To whom God would make known what is the riches of the glory of this **mystery** among the gentiles; which is **Christ in you,** the hope of glory.*

The mystery is that Christ is in you, and so many times we talk about Christ as if He is just in the misty somewhere, some pie in the sky dream. No, and again I say no, Christ is inside the believer. Because of this, I am never trying to be like Christ; I just allow the Christ that is in me to come forth. I am never trying to act like a Christian; I am only a Christian because Christ is in me.

Now I am not playing with semantics, but this is why I say that Christianity is not a religion, but religious people try so hard to be Christians and fail because being like Christ and living out His teachings are impossible without Him. I see this every day and, yes, it hurts my heart because we still think that we can be righteous and come up to God's way without Him, and we can't. This is why God sent His SON. Religion at its best is just a cheap imitation of the real thing, and God is not flattered by it at all, and true Christians are not imitating; they have the real thing and hold a living mystery. What is the mystery? That people see the outward you, but see God on the inside of you. And then you say, I know it is not me, it's a mystery. I can't explain it too well, but Christ is in me. You almost sound crazy to yourself, so you keep it to yourself like Samson did when the strength of God rose up on him and he killed the lion and kept it to himself.

I pray that we understand that when Jesus started talking like this, they said he was crazy, too. We take no credit for the blessings and inheritance that begin to flow in our lives because of this. All of a sudden the things that I could not do I can now, the things that I used to stop at now I finish, the things that I could not overcome now I can because Christ is in me. All the goodness that is in me today is because of Him. We are what we are by the grace of God, and there is nothing that we have that we did not receive.

Colossians 3:1-3 says, *If ye then be risen with Christ, seek those things which are above, where Christ sitteth on the right hand of God. Set your affection on things above, not on things on the earth. For ye are dead, and your life is hid with Christ in God.*

So many people think that when you read this scripture along with Romans chapters six through eight, they leave with the thought that says you are supposed to tell yourself that you are dead. So people walk around telling themselves "I'm dead, I'm dead, you are supposed to be dead, you're dead, die in Jesus' name," you're trying to crucify your own flesh and soul. This is not what God is talking about; you and I must receive by faith what God has done for us through Jesus Christ.

What God is saying is now that you are a believer you have the strength to not only choose but do the right thing. So now you and I choose daily to go God's way. If my wife gets on my nerves, I choose to go God's way, and when I do that by faith, that part of me that wanted to say something back to my wife just died and is replaced with Christ, not just objectively but subjectively now. So the next time my wife does not act like my wife, I won't even have to choose because Christ will just show up because I chose the last time to die in this area because I had the strength to go God's way. Every time you choose God's way you submit to His will and die a little bit more to self. We are supposed to go from submitting to His will to being the will of God, and after we become the will, then we are able to prove the will of God, and you can only prove the will of God when you know the will of God. See Romans 12:2.

When your flesh or your body want to act up, you choose to yield to the life of Christ with in. On the verge of committing some sin and the Holy Spirit says, don't do it, and you say okay, and once you do that here comes the life of Christ, praise God. So now certain issues in your life are not an issue any more because Christ has showed up. A person will say, "I am struggling right there; I am struggling." Well, you said it "YOU" are struggling when what you need to do is yield to the life of Christ within. When you say, "I am struggling with that issue," what you are really saying is subjectively you have not died or yielded to Christ within. So many people shrug the cocoon factor. A boss gets on your last nerve, and God says let it go and you see the grave before you, but you want to say something. Now you have a choice to make. I could use so many different illustrations, but the point is you see the grave you have to make, and you say to God, I am not going to make that grave, but what you don't realize is you are playing with your inheritance. God will even give you the shovel and the pitch fork, and you put the tools down and say I am not going to do it.

We want to mess around with stuff and get close to it, and I am not just talking about sin. It could be to just go and tell someone you apologize but you won't. God could have told you to go on a one-day fast from food, and you won't because you could hear the refrigerator talking to you from your bedroom, and you go and ask it, did it say something. Some of you are saying, come on, you are taking this to serious. Well, I would remind you that Esau lost his birthright over one bowl of soup. When Christ is in our life, we should be bold enough to say about certain things, I will never do that again or that won't happen to me any more, because I can do all things through Christ which strengthens me! God did not create you to fail. He created you in Christ Jesus to be an Overcomer and to have victory in life, and now you and I can say, I have overcome in that area, amen.

Colossians 3:3 says, *For ye **are dead**, and **your life** is **hid** with Christ in God.* If you are dead then your life is hid which means certain things should not bother you any more because by faith in the operation of God you are dead. Colossians 3:4 says, *When Christ, **who** is **our life**, shall appear, then shall ye also appear **with him** in glory.*

It is no longer I that liveth but Christ that liveth in me. What is the recreated human spirit that God is inside of me and me and Him are one. People may only see you, but you have a revelation that it is not you. See Ephesians 2:10. Just say it is not me, but Christ on the inside of me. Remember the scripture says Christ must appear, which means you must allow Him to. We should be able to look in the mirror and say, who is that in there? I see God, He is in me. These are His eyes I see, looking right back at me.

In first Corinthians 15:31 the Apostle Paul said that He died daily. Look at Luke 9:23. It says, *And he* (Jesus) *said to them **all**, If any man will come after me, let him deny himself, and take up his cross **daily**, and follow me.*

This walk is a daily walk of faith, and God is saying that we must deny ourself daily. God did not say self-denial. The right word for self-denial is called ascetic or an ascetic lifestyle, and God is not telling us to do this. This is were most religions miss it because an ascetic life is self-inflicted pain or punishment that we think pleases God or merits His favor in our lives, and this is not what Jesus said. So you have religions out there that don't watch TV, won't eat anything that tastes good, don't own a car, think that it is wrong to marry, or have money, to not be materialistic. I could go on and on, and people think that this is what Christianity is, and it is not.

Jesus did not say self-denial He said to deny yourself daily, which simply means, God, today I choose to go your way in whatever is going on in my life at that time. It could be that I think that the job I am about to take is a good one, but God speaks to me intuitively and says, don't take it. Now I must deny myself and walk by faith and not by sight. A guy cuts in front of me at the store. God says, let it go. Now you have to make a choice to go into the cocoon or act like a child which is the caterpillar stage which is normally something pretty ugly. God might say, turn the TV off today; I want you to spend some time in prayer. Now you have to choose, but that is different from not having a TV at all, or God may say, don't watch that show, and you know why He is telling you don't watch it now. You have to make a choice. This is daily, and it is so fun to have God lead you, guide you and talk to you. Walking by faith daily with God doing what He tells you to do is what takes you through the process, from the caterpillar to the cocoon into the butterfly. And remember that the Holy Spirit will not say anything contrary to the scriptures. He would not say, don't go to church.

We must look up that we can break through so that the glory of God can rest on me and you. I believe the reason most people are afraid of the cross is because they think that God is going to ask them to go to Africa or something, and He might but there are very few that He has called to do something like that. No, most of the time He is just telling us to treat our spouses right, or do the speed limit when you drive. It does not get much deeper than that. Well, it could, but you get the point. What happens when you don't go God's way is you are left to carry life's burden on your own, and for all of us somewhere along the way that luggage is going to get too heavy. But if you go God's way, Christ is there, and with Him you can carry it. I call this the weightless place. When we send people into space, they break earth's atmosphere, and once they do that there is no gravity. It is not that things don't have weight, it's just there you can carry it because once you break through, everything becomes weightless. It is not that anything around you has changed; it is just that you are in the weightless place. Well, so it is in Christ. You are able to deal with life without losing your mind and peace, because in Christ is the weightless place where everything is feather light. Some of you have been carrying your own luggage for too long, and God is saying, Go my way today.

Matthew 11:28-30 says, *Come unto me, all ye that labour and are heavy laden, and I will give you **rest**. Take my yoke upon you,* (go my way) *and learn of me; for I am meek and lowly in heart: and ye shall **find rest** unto your souls, for my yoke is easy, and my burden is light.*

If you have to ask, have I broken through, then you have not broken through, because every astronaut knows when they have broken through, and so will you when you begin to seek those things which are above where Christ sitteth on the right hand of God. It is not that everyone is not carrying luggage, it is just that some of us are in the weightless place or we have allowed the life of Christ to come forward or ,put simply like Jesus said, deny yourself, and take up your cross daily, and follow Him. Some of you have been carrying the luggage of this life on your own long enough and you've been dropping it and spilling it and making a mess of it, and now you are tired of picking it up. Well, you don't have to. Let the Lord carry it for you.

First Peter 5:7 says, *Casting all your care upon him; for he careth for you. Go His way.* Luke 9:24 says, *For whosoever will save his life shall lose it* (going your own way doing your own thing, but getting nowhere): *but whosoever will lose his life for my sake, the same shall save it* (go God's way and be blessed in this life. See Mark 10:28-30).

Don't be ashamed of your heavenly Father or your big brother Jesus because they are not ashamed of you.

Second Corinthians 3:6,14-18 says, (GOD) *Who also hath made us able ministers of the new testament; not of the letter, but of the spirit: for the letter killeth, but the spirit giveth life. But their minds were blinded: for until this day remaineth the same vail untaken away in the reading of the old testament; which vail is done away in Christ. But even unto this day, when Moses is read, the vail is upon their heart. Nevertheless when it shall turn to the Lord, the vail shall be taken away. Now the Lord is that Spirit: and where the Spirit of the Lord is, there is liberty. But we all, with open face beholding as in a glass the glory of the Lord, are changed into the same image from glory to glory, even as by the Spirit of the Lord.*

People of God, we must first turn to the Lord on our own with a pure heart. When we do this, the Lord gives us liberty which is not the right to dance in church which I am not against, but that is not what he is talking about. No, what he is talking about is the emancipation proclamation of your spirit, soul and body to be truly liberated or set free. For whom the son sets free is free indeed. Our freedom does not come from the government or any other organization; no true freedom comes from God alone. This happens as we look at the Lord. We are changed progressively (and this word changed is that Greek word again, metamorphoo). Change comes when we look at ourselves through God's mirror which is the Word of God, as we read it and meditate it under the anointing of the Holy Spirit. The book of James calls the Word of God the perfect law of liberty or the only law in the world when read in the spirit that does not bind but frees, for in God nothing is impossible. The emphasis in God and in life is change. This cannot be avoided. The question is, what kind of change are you experiencing in your life? We are supposed to go from one level of glory to another level of glory. This happens by the living God and not by a set of dead rules! If you and I do not change, then something is wrong and we will become hypocritical to ourselves and others while we are on this Christian journey. We should not be the same tomorrow as we are today; we are constantly becoming.

Husbands and Wives will say to each other, "Why don't you change?" and that spouse will say, "Well, you married me this way." Well, that does not mean that you have to stay that way; you can grow, you can change by the power of God. If you are 35 and you act the same way you did at 18, something is wrong. Those of us that say I know the Lord, and I am filled with the Spirit but there is no change, the Bible says that all you have is a form of godliness, but you deny the power. Because if God was in your life the way that you say, you would see change. The only being in the universe that is not subject to change is GOD, for He said, I am the LORD and I CHANGE NOT. The book of Hebrews says Jesus Christ, the SAME yesterday, today and forever.

The reason God does not change is because He is perfect in all of His ways, and you cannot improve on perfection. God is not trying to change you into a better CEO or better preacher. No, He is only changing you into the image of His SON, and that's what I want. I don't want to preach a better message; I just want to be a son. I don't want a deeper sermon; I want a deeper life. It is out of a deeper life there comes a deeper message, the better preacher or outstanding CEO.

There was a person in the Gospel of John named Lazarus who died, but the people thought that if Jesus could have gotten there earlier that he would have lived. So in John 11:23-26, Jesus said unto Martha, Lazarus's sister, *Jesus saith unto her, Thy brother shall rise again.*

Martha saith unto him, I know that he shall rise again in the resurrection at the last day. Jesus said unto her, **I AM the resurrection, and the life:** *he that believeth in me, though he were dead, yet shall he live: And whosoever liveth and believeth in me shall never die. Believest thou this?*

You see, people of God, Martha thought that resurrection was an event, and so do most of you, but resurrection is not an event. Resurrection is a person! The power that raises the dead dwells in you now if you are a believer.

Romans 8:10-11 says, *And if Christ be in you, the body is dead because of sin; but the Spirit is life because of righteousness. But if the Spirit of him that raised up Jesus from the dead dwell in you, he that raised up Christ from the dead shall also quicken* (make alive) *your mortal bodies by* **his Spirit that dwelleth in you.**

God wants you to die to self that He can raise you up in newness of life by His Spirit that dwells in you.

Second Corinthians 5:14-18 says, *For the* **love** *of Christ constraineth us; because we thus judge, that if one died for all, then were all dead: and that he died for all, that they which live should not henceforth* **live unto themselves, but unto him which died for them, and rose again.** *Wherefore henceforth know we no man after the flesh: yea, though we have known Christ after the flesh, yet now henceforth know we him no more. Therefore if any man be* **in Christ,** *he is a* **new creature:** *old things are passed away; behold,* **all things are become new.** *And* **all things are of God,** *who hath reconciled us to himself by Jesus Christ, and hath given to us the ministry of reconciliation.*

When we yield to Christ within, we are changed and our change is of God, and it is also a change that can only happen by God. As we understand this, we too will stop looking at and judging people from their outward appearance and see their hearts and begin to release real life that helps. The reason most of us will not give up our lives or our way is because we cannot see ourselves alive unto and into something so much better and, believe me, when you go God's way, you are always going into something better than what you had or could do. And I know that this is hard for some of us to believe, but that is why we walk by faith and not by sight.

People of God, I share all of this to say that there is a middle ground between childhood and sonship that we must all partake of, and that is the cocoon factor. We must choose to die, which simply means I am going to obey God and go His way every day. This plays a vital part in our maturity, and we all know the areas of our life that God is telling us to deal with. This is deeper than just money because there are people that have money but they are miserable, people that have positions but have no peace and I pray go God's way.

LAST WORDS

I PRAY that this book will help usher in the Anointing of God for a new millennium. As we approach the 21st century I trust God that we all come into our inheritance as sons. I pray that we all would repent of those things that we know have hindered God's process for our lives. That we enter into this next millennium with a fresh start and a new beginning, knowing that it is never too late for God to bring our dreams and visions to pass. I pray that we go forward with fresh fire, understanding that it is never to late for God, that He is able to raise up and restore just as he did with Lazarus. There may be things that stink in your life like Lazarus did since he was dead for four days, but I tell you of a truth, people of God, Jesus is able to remove the smell and resurrect your dream and repair your vision and cause you to fly. And this is my prayer for you, that you fly, like an eagle in the sky. So mount up on the current of God's love and say, I trust the Lord to take me all the way. I still believe in miracles, I still believe that dreams come true, the ones that God has for me and the ones that He has for you. So approach this next year without doubt and without fear, and know that Jesus is closer than close. He is very near, call upon Him now. Believe me, He will hear, just cast all your care upon Jesus. He will make your life crystal clear. Now stay true to yourself and true to Him, for I have confidence that you and I win.

Let us pray.
Lord, I thank you that I am one that you have given the
POWER TO BECOME.

God bless all that read this book.
God loves you and I do, too!

For more information or speaking engagements on Apostle Cornelius Sanders, please call or write us at:

Revelation Ministries Christian Church
10330 E. Harry St.
Wichita, KS 67207

Telephone Number
1/316/685-3236

Rev. H.h Church
474 Havenwood Drive
Sumter S.C. 29130